T0149394

SPIRIT
OF THE
SKY WALKERS

PHILIP I. MOYNIHAN

SPIRIT OF THE SKY WALKERS

iUniverse books may be ordered through booksellers or by contacting:

iUniverse
1663 Liberty Drive
Bloomington, IN 47403
www.iuniverse.com
1-800-Authors (1-800-288-4677)

ISBN: 978-1-5320-8880-3 (sc)
ISBN: 978-1-5320-8879-7 (e)

Library of Congress Control Number: 2019918679

Print information available on the last page.

iUniverse rev. date: 01/09/2020

CONTENTS

For Gordon and Shirley Hughes

Thanks for introducing us to the world of aviation and for sharing so many fantastic flying adventures with us

PROLOGUE

Flying is not for everyone. In fact, I would venture to say that a significant majority of the population is terrified by it. Many people experience dizzying sensations like vertigo when confronting high places. Without a secure hold or stable footing, they have a very real fear of falling. We humans are ground animals. We evolved knowing that "up" is the blue above us and "down" is always below – the solid ground.

But none of these references is valid in the sky. The sky is a foreign environment, devoid of any such illusion; and when our airplane enters the clouds, we find this state dramatically so. Without spatial reference, many an unfortunate pilot has looked *up* at the ground.

Flying has intrigued our species' genus since the first *Homo erectus* watched a bird wing its way across the sky. If only we could follow it – drift through the sky, do what it does, go where it goes. Yet it would take well over several million years before we could truly shed the bonds of gravity and join it.

For those of us who have actually broken these chains and taken flight, it's a magical experience. It's a feeling of ultimate freedom, unbounded by gravity's constraints, flowing unrestricted through the fluid ether. It's a sensation that defies description through normal prose, as words alone, with their limited ability to portray the ethereal enchantment wrought in this alien environment, are inadequate. But when augmented by poetry, with its elusive subtlety and metaphoric abstractions, one can begin to understand its attraction.

The anecdotes portrayed in the ensuing stories are actual recounts of our flying adventures accumulated over three decades. Each chapter of this book is introduced with a poem. I felt that starting with a poem would aid the reader in acquiring a more intuitive feel for this unnatural environment. The intent of these poems, poems about flying and the spirit of flying, is to help set the mood for the subject of the chapter and to help the reader viscerally accept this alien setting.

The aim of each poem is to capture the sensation and awe of being by oneself in the cockpit; to be like the bird, adrift and soaring alone above the world; to see what the bird sees; to feel what the bird feels. For a moment at least, as if caught in a daydream, the lone pilot is walking in the sky. He is a Sky Walker.

But to the nonflying public, the terminology used by pilots – and reflected in these poems – may be confusing. Like all hobbies and professions, aviation has its own special language, and becoming familiar with that language is part of the acceptance of this new world.

The narration following each poem – whether it be a brief history of flight relevant to the subject of the poem or an anecdote or short story from our own flight experiences – will help define and clarify the meanings of these new expressions. After reading the poems, read the ensuing prose. Many of the unfamiliar terms will be explained, either through direct definition or through the context of the anecdotes presented.

Then return and reread the poem. You will likely have a renewed perspective. You too, at least in your mind's eye, will become a Sky Walker.

CHAPTER 1

IF ONLY I COULD FLY!

When I was a wee lad
I used to lie
On my back in the clover
And look up at the sky.
I would watch the clouds pass
And the birds soar by.

The breeze on my face
I felt where I'd lie
Whispered to the trees
Till their leaves cast a sigh.

I daydreamed for hours
As the sun traced the sky,
While clouds piled in bundles
And the mist would rise high.

The eagles screamed loudly
And the blackbirds would cry.
My world was the ether
From where I would lie.
What wonders would I know
If only I could fly!

The wind on my wings
Would carry me high!
I could roam through the heavens,
I could touch the sky!

I'd jump over the moon
As the stars shot by.
I'd sweep over the fields
Like a dragonfly.

I'd scream with the eagles!
I'd float through the sky
On a gossamer web
That'd slowly drift by.
All wonders I would know
If only I could fly!

"If Only I Could Fly!" is the dream of virtually every young lad at some time during his childhood. I was fortunate to have grown up on a farm in central Vermont where, as a nine-year-old, I could spend an occasional lazy summer afternoon wandering out into a clover field and engaging in this very daydream. There was sparse human population in the local region, and that allowed the nonhuman inhabitants like birds to relax and play. The clover was cool and fresh smelling, and the birds would dart about chasing insects and one another. To those of us who to this day are prone to daydreaming, it was a magical experience.

Flying has been a dream and desire of humans for literally thousands of years. Virtually every culture on the planet can recount stories buried in legend or myth of connections with the sky and the primal urge to take part. After all, the sun and moon and stars were high above us. How did they get there? And the birds – what graceful creatures gliding effortlessly through the air. Why can't humans be part of that?

We humans have been envious of the birds for as long as we have been able to recognize their ability to sever the bonds of gravity and climb gracefully through the sky. And it's only been within the past instant of time in our existence as a species that we have been able to join them. But our collective mythologies are filled with examples of the subliminal desire to do so.

Everyone, for instance, is familiar with the story in Greek mythology of the fate of Icarus, the son of Daedalus. Imprisoned on Crete by King Minos, Daedalus and Icarus planned to escape by flying off the island with wings to be constructed by Daedalus, who was a master craftsman. Because he made the wings of feathers and wax, Daedalus cautioned Icarus not to fly too close to the sun lest the sun's heat melt the wax. But once in the air, euphoria overcame Icarus, and he ignored the caution. Instead, he soared high into the sky and came too close to the sun. The sun melted the wax, causing his feathers to fly away. With his wings gone, Icarus fell into the sea and drowned.

But what may not be as familiar to most of us, yet is pervasive throughout the world's cultural histories, is the richness of stories and mythologies of not only flight itself but also of mystical humanlike beings capable of flight. The characters in these stories often assume human form and fulfill a niche fantasy of a trait that reflects some segment of human nature symbolic of the local culture. Ancient Mesopotamian and Egyptian gods are often depicted with wings. The supreme god of Zoroastrianism, Ahura Mazda, is exhibited on royal inscriptions by Achaemenid kings as a winged entity.[1] In ancient Hebrew carvings, angels and cherubs typically were portrayed with wings. But wings were not an absolute flight necessity for the ancient Greek or Roman gods. Even the angels of biblical references didn't become equipped with wings until the Middle Ages.

The Valkyries from Norse mythology are another example of winged messengers. They were female figures typically depicted bearing wings and wearing winged helmets and who resided in Asgard, one of the Nine Worlds in the Norse version of heaven that was ruled by Odin and Frigg (or Frija, in Old High German).[2] The Valkyries would fly down from Asgard on horseback and choose from among the warriors who would live or die on the battlefield. They would then select half of those and carry the favored slain warriors to Valhalla, the Great Hall of Odin, where these warriors would be served mead, the nectar of the gods. These favorites would join Odin in battle during Ragnarok, the battle for the end of the world. The reflection that results from the Valkyries' beating their swords against their shields is said to appear in the sky as the northern lights.

Sixteenth-century Chinese texts make reference to Sun Wukong, the Monkey King born from a stone, and tell of his travels on a golden cloud.[3] Although he himself did not possess wings, his powers made him capable of flying anywhere in the

---

[1] Radu Cristian, "Ahura Mazda," Ancient History Encyclopedia, last modified March 13, 2017, https://www.ancient.eu/Ahura_Mazda/.
[2] Wikipedia, s.v. "Valkyrie," last modified July 21, 2019, https://en.wikipedia.org/wiki/Valkyrie.
[3] Wikipedia. "Sun Wukong," last modified August 1, 2019. https://en.wikipedia.org/wiki/Sun_Wukong.

world on his golden cloud. He also had other powers that gave him tremendous strength, including sufficient power to defeat all the armies of the Jade Emperor. And once on his cloud, he had the ability to accelerate its speed until it reached God Speed. These stories trace their origin as far back as the Song Dynasty, which existed from the tenth through the thirteenth centuries.

Japanese folklore mentions the Tengu, a type of Shinto god possessing both human and avian characteristics and capable of taking the form of birds of prey.[4] The beaks in earlier renditions of Tengus were later replaced with unnaturally long human noses. While originally depicted as a demon and harbinger of war, its image later softened into that of a protector of the forests and mountains. Although various incarnations of the Tengu have been referenced in Japanese literature from as early as 720 CE, many Japanese scholars have speculated that the image and flight characteristics of the Tengu may have been derived from the Hindu eagle deity, the Garuda, and introduced to Japan through Buddhism.

The Garuda is a legendary flight figure typically depicted as a winged human with the head of a bird and is manifested in Hindu and Southeast Asian mythologies.[5] Often considered as a protector with the power to go anywhere, it is occasionally portrayed in association with the Hindu god Vishnu, the Protector, and as Vishnu's mount. Known as the enemy of the serpent Naga, the Garuda represents force, speed, and military might, sweeping down on vanquished armies as it would onto the Naga. Krishna, the eighth avatar of Vishnu, is said to have carried the image of Garuda on his banner. Today, the Garuda is not only represented

---

[4] Wikipedia. "Tengu," last modified July 12, 2019. https://en.wikipedia.org/wiki/Tengu.

[5] Williams, George M. 2008. "Handbook of Hindu Mythology." Oxford: Oxford University Press. Pp 138-139.

in the insignias of many Southeast Asian countries, such as India, Thailand, and Cambodia, but it is also the name of an airline – Garuda Indonesia is the official airline of Indonesia.

Another anthropomorphic being capable of flight is the harpie.[6] The harpies have their origin in ancient Greek mythology and were initially depicted with the body of a bird but the head of a maiden. Considered to be vicious and cruel, their name means "snatcher" or "swift robber." With their long, sharp claws, they would steal food and generally cause mischief, and they would carry souls to the underworld. Their assumption of a human form may have originally been derived from the destructive character of strong winds, as they very likely were initially anthropomorphized as wind spirits. In later Roman times, they were depicted as women with wings, eliminating the bird body. Although Roman literature referenced their ugliness, with the example of Ovid describing them as human vultures, the pottery of the time was much kinder to them. Nonetheless, people intent upon evildoing were cautioned lest they be carried off by "the hounds of Zeus" – the harpies.

Many ancient flight fantasies were adaptations and extrapolations of the cultural understandings of familiar entities. As an example, an epic poem by the Persian poet Ferdowsi tells of the ancient Persian king Kay Kavus, who had fashioned a flying craft that was carried by specially trained eagles.[7] The craft was a throne with an upward-pointing pole attached to each corner. The eagles were tied to the bottom of each pole, and pieces of meat were hung at the top and out of reach of the eagles. As the eagles attempted to reach the meat, they would lift the throne, causing

---

[6] Wikipedia. "Harpy," last modified July 5, 2019. https://en.wikipedia.org/wiki/Harpy.

[7] Wikipedia. "Kay Kavus," last modified May 26, 2019. https://en.wikipedia.org/wiki/Kay_Kāvus.

it to fly. Legend has it that with this configuration, Kay Kavus flew all the way to China.

Then there's the story of the Celtic king of the Britons, King Bladud, who at a time somewhere between the middle of the eighth century and fifth century BCE is said to have fashioned wings of feathers and attempted to fly from a tower in New Troy to the Temple of Apollo in what is now London.[8] His maiden flight was unsuccessful.

And of course everyone knows the story from *One Thousand and One Nights* of the young Arabian prince Husain who traveled to India and bought a magic carpet. He was told that if a person sat on the carpet and thought of a place he or she would like to go, the carpet would instantly take the person there. Most magic carpet stories, however, involve carpets that actually fly, rather than instantly teleporting their passengers. Such stories of magic carpets are found far back in antiquity, even in ancient Hebrew legends. King Solomon was said to have had a massive flying carpet made of green silk that measured sixty miles by sixty miles. The carpet would be caught by the wind and sail rapidly through the air.[9]

Flying carpets are also mentioned in Russian folktales in the stories of the witch Baba Yaga, although fables of Baba Yaga more commonly tell of her flying close to the ground in a mortar while her right hand wields a pestle, which she used as a rudder.[10] She swept away her tracks with a silver birch broom in her left hand, and she lived deep in the forest in a hut that was difficult to find. Winds would blow, trees would groan, and leaves would

---

[8] Pioneers of Aviation. "King Bladud," last modified January 11, 2013. https://av8rblog.wordpress.com/2013/01/11/king-bladud/.

[9] Wikipedia. "Magic Carpet," last modified June 21, 2019. https://en.wikipedia.org/wiki/Magic_carpet.

[10] Wikipedia. "Baba Yaga," last modified July 15, 2019. https://en.wikipedia.org/wiki/Baba_Yaga.

rustle whenever she appeared. People sought her counsel as the all-knowing, all-seeing, all-wise shaman.

But less known from ancient legends of flight are tales like the stories of the Vimana from Sanskrit epics and Hindu texts.[11] The Vimana were various forms of mythological flying chariots, thrones, or even palaces that glided through the air, powered by thought. Of these flying palaces or chariots of the gods, the Pushpaka Vimana of King Ravana, the demon king of Lanka, is likely the most referenced example. King Ravana is typically depicted with ten heads.

We humans have dreamed about flying for thousands of years and have invented exotic mythologies of mysterious beings capable of taking flight. We waited a very long time before we finally were able to actually throw aside gravity's chains and take to the air in person. And now it's no longer even necessary to be a pilot to do so. All the average person need do is to buy a ticket on a commercial airline, select a window seat, and settle in to enjoy the view.

But with all the above as an introduction, exactly how did Penny and I happen to take up flying, one might ask. That in and of itself is an interesting story, and it all began during Memorial Day weekend in 1985. We were invited to accompany our friends Gordon and Shirley Hughes on a flight from Van Nuys, California, to Alamos, Mexico, in Gordon's Cessna 182. We had no idea as to what to expect when we left Van Nuys on that beautiful spring day, but we were looking forward to the adventure. Everything about that flight was perfect – customs processing went smoothly, and the weather cooperated for the entire weekend. In the year we took this trip, Alamos was still a

---

[11] Wikipedia. "Vimana," last modified June 23, 2019. https://en.wikipedia.org/wiki/Vimana.

fairly small town, located near the southern border of the Mexican state of Sonora.

After we cleared Mexican customs, our flight path took us over Copper Canyon, a canyon area in Mexico that rivals the Grand Canyon in depth. Gordon circled over it to give us all a good view of the canyon from the air. I was sitting in the right front seat, and occasionally along the way Gordon would let me manipulate the yoke and rudders. *I could come to like this!* I thought. I have always had an interest in aviation. In fact, my undergraduate degree is in aeronautical engineering. But with all the priorities we were dealing with at that time merely getting through our daily lives, only rarely had I thought about taking flying lessons. And I subconsciously suspected that Penny would likely not be interested, as she had never mentioned it, and we tend to do those kinds of endeavors together.

Once we arrived at Alamos, Gordon circled over the town as a signal to any available taxi drivers that we would be landing shortly and would need a ride. That maneuver was apparently common among aviators, we learned. I don't remember much about the runway at Alamos, other than that it was quite narrow. If it was paved, the asphalt looked old and worn, or possibly it could have been hard-packed dirt. I never paid attention to those details at that time. And besides, Gordon took care of all the aviation things during that trip. While we were parking the plane, the taxi showed up.

We had a very good time in Alamos and met several most interesting people, many of whom were American expatriates. Of particular note was a British woman whose late husband had flown in the Royal Air Force (RAF) during the Battle of Britain. He had recently died and was buried in the local cemetery, granting Alamos, Mexico, as the final resting place of a British RAF pilot responsible for the defense of London during the dark days of World War II. She told us that the entire town had turned out for his funeral.

On our return from Alamos, it was Penny's turn in the right seat. Gordon had mentioned earlier that our plans called for our stopping in Guaymas on our way back to meet up with the Santa Monica Flying Club, which was having a fly-in there that weekend, and we would be spending the night at the same hotel. Since Gordon's plane was based in Santa Monica, he was a member of that club. For the first leg of the flight, Penny sat politely, keeping her hands off everything. Being so close to all the controls was a new experience for her.

We landed at the Guaymas airport without incident, took care of the airplane, and got a ride to our hotel. After we checked in, we caught up with the flying club members who were already in the hotel dining room.

The hotel dining room was quite large, with numerous tables that were already set up for dinner when we walked in, and we were invited to join them. With likely very few exceptions, virtually everyone in the room was a licensed pilot, so the majority of the conversations centered on flying. The magic that sparked Penny's interest in aviation happened during this dinner party. With the flowing wine and boisterous voices, Penny noted that these were ordinary people who happened to also be pilots. Aviators didn't wear capes and possess superpowers. Flying an airplane didn't necessarily require that one be superhuman. As the party was drawing to an end, Penny was talking with Shirley, and I overheard her say, "If these people can learn to fly, then so can I." That was it! That was all the spark that I needed to follow up.

Before we left Guaymas the next day, I asked Gordon if he would let Penny ride in the right seat once more and somewhere along the way let her manipulate the controls so that she could get a feel for how an airplane handles. He was quite agreeable with that suggestion and even proposed the notion that she might come to like it. So that's what we did. Gordon let her take the controls several times during our flight home. One event that I remember in particular was when she was executing a climb but did it so steeply that she almost stalled the airplane. But that didn't disturb her at all. It was fun! She was hooked.

Twelve days after we returned from that trip, we met with a flight instructor at the El Monte airport to start flight lessons. We walked into the flight school office that Saturday afternoon, and a flight instructor, Eddie, was sitting there with his feet on the desk. We informed him that we both were interested in taking flight lessons and that we would like to begin right then. He was receptive and told us that we were welcome and that the school could take us on, but on that particular afternoon, all the school's planes were out. However, we could set up a time on a different day, and he would ensure that a plane would be reserved.

Then he gave us the specifics on the lessons – what they would involve, the type of plane we would use, how long they would likely take, how much they would cost, and then some. As he was talking, he made a suggestion that resonated well with both of us. He suggested that we consider team training. For team training both of us would fly simultaneously with the instructor, but one of us would be in the "hot seat" to the left of the instructor, while the other would be in the back seat watching. After each lesson, which would take about an hour, we would land and change positions. The person who just finished the lesson would go to the back, while the observer would move to the hot seat. We would then take off again, and the instructor would repeat the same lesson. This allowed the first person to reinforce the lesson just learned while sitting in the back, while the second person could apply what he or she had just observed. Since this procedure would be perfect for us, we immediately opted for that selection. All of this school's training planes were the high-wing, nonretractable-gear Cessnas, and most new students started lessons in the two-place Cessna 152. But because we were going to be team training, we would start with the four-place Cessna 172. Next, we scheduled our first lesson. The first available time period in which all of us, plus the airplane, were available was after work on the following Thursday.

As we left the flight school and were walking back to the car, we discussed what had just happened and the incredible adventure that was being laid out in front of us. We were now on our way. Then Penny became serious and expressed both a complaint and a concern. She indicated that during the entire time we were talking with the flight instructor, she had observed that he had only talked to me. He didn't talk to her once, implying to her that he thought she was likely not all that interested. I looked at her momentarily, and then I told her that this would not be a problem. When we show up for our first lesson on Thursday, she would be first up – the first one in the left seat receiving the very first lesson. That would tell the instructor immediately that she was a serious candidate.

That following Thursday, June 13, 1985, exactly seventeen days after our return from Alamos, we met with Eddie, our flight instructor, to begin receiving formal flight lessons in the left seat for the first time. And the rest, as they say, is history.

Our primary flight training proceeded quite normally. We practiced landings; we did stalls; we did climbs and descents; we did unusual attitudes; we took ground school; we soloed; and we did cross-country flights. We did everything the law required to prepare us to venture safely into an unnatural environment. Finally, we were ready for our check-ride.

The check-ride is an oral and practical exam given by a local Federal Aviation Administration (FAA) designated examiner who determines whether a fledgling pilot is competent to be the sole manipulator of the controls of an airplane that may have passengers aboard. It can be a very intimidating experience, but we were ready. And by some strange coincidence, as the Fates would have it, on June 13, 1986 – exactly one year to the day after we had our first-ever flight lesson with Eddie – we each flew a two-place Cessna 152 to the Fullerton Airport to meet with the FAA flight examiner. Both of us passed! On that day, when the ride was over, we each had accumulated sixty-six flight hours. We were on our way!

We spent the majority of the following year renting various aircraft, checking out what we felt most comfortable flying. We transitioned to a low-wing airplane and found that we liked that specific concept. But as we coordinated and maneuvered through the realm of rental aircraft, we encountered several frustrations. We would often find something amiss with the plane we rented, even if we had rented the same one a few days earlier. We have encountered loose landing struts, missing radios, nonfunctioning instruments, and many other anomalies. We finally decided it was time to consider buying our own airplane.

Once again, luck was with us. Our friend Gordon Hughes at that time had recently accepted a new job in Silicon Valley and was looking to relocate his recently purchased Mooney from Santa Monica to San Jose. But he needed a hangar, and none was available. Then he learned of a space that could be made available if somehow the airplane presently in it, which was for sale, could be relocated. He jumped at this opportunity and bought the airplane, knowing that he could probably resell it. At the very least he could relocate it and free up the hangar space.

Gordon's airplane shuffling was taking place unbeknownst to us, and furthermore he had no knowledge that we had started seriously looking to buy an airplane. Within a month or so after we had started looking for available airplanes, Gordon called us and told us what he had just done. He had an airplane for sale at a good price. We told him of the weird coincidence of his call and said yes, we were interested. The only downside for us at the time was that the airplane he had for sale was a Mooney. Up to that point, we had been looking to buy something along the line of a Piper, a low-wing with fixed landing gear.

A Mooney is considered a complex airplane in that it has retractable landing gear and a constant-speed propeller. The operation of a constant-speed propeller allows the pilot to set the engine at a predetermined revolutions per minute (RPM), and the propeller blade pitch will automatically adjust to maintain that RPM. Up to that time in our flying career, we had very limited experience with a complex airplane. Furthermore, a pilot is required to undergo a special checkout to transition into that specific class of aircraft. Virtually all the planes we had flown had been fixed-gear and fixed-pitch propellers. As a further complication, this particular Mooney had manually operated landing gear, which was an unknown issue all unto itself. But after discussing these options for a short while, we concluded that we should give it a try. We were confident that we could find a flight instructor who could check us out in a complex airplane and help us get familiar with this one.

So we arranged for a test excursion to St. George, Utah, for the upcoming Fourth of July weekend. Gordon and Shirley in their Mooney; and John, the original owner of the Mooney being demoed, and his wife in the demo Mooney would all fly into El Monte. We would meet everyone there and bring them to our house, where everyone would stay the night. After breakfast the following day we all would leave for St. George. Penny and I would ride with John, who would pilot the demo Mooney to show us its operations, while his wife rode with Gordon and Shirley. This scenario worked out very well. It was a long-enough trip to give us a good feel for the airplane. And while at St. George, John had both Penny and me do touch-and-goes at the St. George Airport, which at that time was located atop a mesa. It has since been relocated to the valley. This gave us great preliminary experience for making the approach to landing and operating the manual landing gear. Furthermore, we had to deal with crosswinds that day, which was an opportunity for us to obtain a very good feel for how the airplane handled under those conditions. We also learned that a Mooney lands quite differently from the planes we had been flying to date. One has to fly the Mooney all the way to the ground.

By the time we returned home, we were feeling very confident and told Gordon that he had a deal. In July 1987 we bought the Mooney. John and his wife joined Gordon and Shirley in their Mooney for the return to San Jose, leaving us with our "new" Mooney parked at El Monte.

Now the fun began. We inquired at our original flight school at El Monte to find a flight instructor who would be willing to check us out in a complex airplane, and within the next couple of weeks it was happening. And very shortly thereafter we informed our instructor that since he was certified to train instrument students, we wanted to continue onward for an instrument rating. An instrument rating would afford us many more flight options by enabling us to fly under Instrument Flight Rules (IFR) in bad weather. More importantly, an IFR rating would allow us to break through the low ceilings that are common in the springtime throughout the Los Angeles Basin.

A special certification is required of all flight instructors who will be training students for an IFR rating where the student would be flying under Instrument Flight Rules. They hold the title of a Certified Flight Instructor Instrument, or CFII. In the vernacular of the flight-training world, they are called a Double I.

Our instructor said he was willing to take us on as students for this new venture, but he suggested that we consider doing our training in a simpler airplane. We voted against that idea. We were going to be doing our future flying in this Mooney, so we figured we should become as familiar with it as possible, even if it took us longer to get our next rating. He agreed to this condition, and we were on our way.

An IFR rating is a virtual necessity for anyone who wishes to fly with any regularity in and out of the Los Angeles Basin. The reason for this is that the Basin, as it's called, is surrounded on three sides by very high mountains and borders the ocean on the fourth. The southerly flow of the Alaska current off the coastline brings with it very cold water. Because of the Mediterranean climate of the Los Angeles Basin, every spring these mountains contribute to a temperature inversion that traps moist marine air that forms a stable overcast sky across the entire area. This steady but persistent overcast is referred to as May Gray and June Gloom. Typically, the cloud layer is not very dense, often only a couple of hundred feet thick. And usually it's not very high, maybe three or four thousand feet above ground. But to the noninstrument-rated pilot, it's an iron ceiling that cannot be penetrated. Without an instrument rating, one is essentially grounded. But once on top of this layer, the visibility is virtually unlimited. If we were ever to expect to fly during that time of year, it would be imperative that we get an instrument rating.

As we continued on with our instrument flight training, we became more familiar with our new Mooney and felt much more comfortable with its operation and idiosyncrasies. Partway through our tutoring, however, our original instructor left for a better career opportunity and arranged for us to transfer to another Double I, with whom we finished our program. The remainder of our IFR instructions proceeded fairly routinely, and on June 14, 1989, almost exactly four years after our first-ever flight instruction, we were ready for our instrument check-rides. My check-ride would occur on the fourteenth, and Penny's would follow a day later.

Our instrument check-rides did not proceed without a hitch, however. The problem was not with our having done something wrong, as we both successfully passed. In fact, we both passed rather handily. The glitch we encountered was with the airplane radios. Ours at the time of our check-ride were fairly old.

Airplanes are all about redundancy, and that is especially important when it comes to navigation and communication. Virtually all general-aviation aircraft are equipped with two radios for communication and two very high frequency (VHF) omnidirectional range (VOR) receivers for navigation. The VOR receivers are themselves radios that enable the pilot to navigate along the radio beams or radials emitted by the VOR transmitters. One of the skills the examiner would look for from the pilot taking an IFR check-ride is how well the examinee coordinates between each radio and VOR receiver to successfully communicate and navigate. A worst-case scenario for the examinee would be if there were only one radio and one VOR receiver available in the airplane during the check-ride.

In the world of perverse laws of the universe, Murphy's Law reigns above all others. While I was performing the engine run-up tests with the FAA-designated examiner, Margaret Lawson, in the right seat immediately prior to my check-ride, one radio and one VOR both failed. When these failures occurred, Margaret immediately asked me if I wanted to cancel the check-ride to have these instruments repaired and reschedule, or if I would prefer to continue with only one radio and VOR receiver. At some time during the check-ride, she would likely fail one of these functions anyway as a partial-panel test by putting a sticker over it and disallowing its use. All instrument pilots are expected to successfully navigate and control the aircraft without all the instruments and radios functioning. Without hesitating, I opted to continue. The only real concern I had was that if we lost either of the other two capabilities, we would definitely have to cancel the check-ride. But so far they were working, and we took off.

I should point out that during an instrument check-ride, the examinee is wearing a hood that allows him to see only the instrument panel of the airplane. He cannot see outside. The whole point of instrument flying is maintaining situational awareness from information provided by the instruments alone. Having only one radio for communication was not overly inconvenient since we were in constant contact with the air traffic controllers, and they told us what frequencies to use. However, having only one VOR receiver required a major exercise in mental agility.

One of the skills to be demonstrated during any IFR check ride is the VOR intersection hold. A VOR intersection is where a specific radial signal from one VOR transmitter crosses a specific radial signal of a different VOR. Here's an example of how such a hold might go. The traffic controller might say, "Hold on the Paradise 278-degree radial at the Pomona 164-degree radial, right turns." Executing a hold like this with two VOR receivers is fairly straightforward. One would dial in the frequency for the Paradise VOR transmitter, set the required radial on one receiver, and dial in the Pomona VOR and set its radial on the other. To find the intersection, the pilot flies in the direction required to center the needle of one of the VORs and then follows that radial until the needle centers on the other. When both needles are centered, the pilot is at the intersection, where he or she begins executing right turns.

If the aircraft is equipped with only one VOR receiver, however, this procedure is much more complex, as now everything must be done in series. First, the pilot has to dial in the frequency of one of the VOR transmitters and set the radial to see how much the needle displaces. Then he has to repeat this same process with the second VOR transmitter. Whichever transmitter has the lesser needle displacement is the one he would first choose to fly to and center on. Once that needle is centered and the airplane is on the correct radial, he would then dial in the second VOR transmitter and proceed to center that needle while maintaining the correct aircraft heading by using the directional gyro, or DG. When that VOR needle centers, he is at the desired intersection. He then makes his right turn and tracks outbound while dialing in the original VOR transmitter signal so he can find the correct radial and center the needle when he tracks inbound to the intersection once more. And he repeats the redialing procedure with the second VOR transmitter so he can refind the intersection. This goes on for as long as he is in the hold. That's what I did on that day and what Penny did on the following day. We were very busy! But we were successful. Penny and I both were now instrument-rated private pilots.

And so it came to pass, as we will witness even more in the ensuing chapters, Penny and I both broke gravity's bonds and learned to fly. Through fortunate circumstance and the help and encouragement of friends, we both became pilots. And then, by ourselves, we were able to venture into an environment that the vast majority of the human race could only dream of for centuries. We took what were to become the first steps into a world of adventure that would extend over three decades. And we never looked back.

So the daydream of that nine-year-old lad lying in the clover staring at the sky on a balmy Vermont afternoon finally did become a reality. At last, he was able to fly. And this experience certainly opened his world to unimagined wonders where he did indeed scream with the eagles and float through the sky. He outdid Icarus. He is now in the company of Tengu and the Valkyries. He has his own flying carpet. He became a Sky Walker.

CHAPTER 2

THE GIFT OF WINGS

From my cockpit
    I can see the whole world before me.

I see the mottled farmlands
    With their tiny streams
        And dotted ponds.

I see the craggy mountains
    And glacial floes,
        And their tortured passes

Dipping into the green valleys
    With their meandering rivers
        And sandy river banks.

I see the multicolored mesas
Cut by the wind
And washed by an ancient ocean
Long since passed.

I see clouds
Piled like downy cushions,
So soft you could jump into them,

With mountain peaks protruding above
Like Titan gods
Guarding their realm.

I see the towns
With their jumble of houses
Crouching under their rooftops,

As if to escape
The angry wrath
Of some invisible force.

I can see forever!
From yesterday
All the way past tomorrow!

For I –
Like the raven,
Like the eagle,
Like the condor –

I have
The Gift of Wings!
I can fly!

I wrote "The Gift of Wings" well over two decades ago, with special apologies to Richard Bach for having borrowed its title from his book of the same name that he published in 1970. Bach is probably best known for his excellent story, "Jonathan Livingston Seagull."

Flying in a small airplane offers a vantage point that one doesn't experience through commercial flight in large airliners. In a large airliner, one is typically at thirty-plus-thousand feet, well above any altitude where one can come to appreciate the details of the terrain below. But in a small airplane, flying at an altitude of three or four thousand feet above the surface, one is presented with an entirely new perspective of the surrounding environment. One sees new details of the world from a viewpoint previously unimagined. It's that viewpoint that "The Gift of Wings" attempts to describe.

Penny and I have flown all over North America in fair weather and foul, north of the Arctic Circle and south to Puerto Vallarta, Mexico; we've soared over the Pacific Coast from Cabo San Lucas at the lower tip of Baja California, to Vancouver, Canada; we have followed the Yukon River in Alaska, the Fraser River in British Columbia, and the Mississippi; we've flown the length of the Atlantic Coast from Maine to Georgia; and we have landed at countless small airports throughout the interior of the country. We have experienced tailwinds so strong that we could point the nose down and surf the mountain waves, and we have experienced the "Headwinds from Hell," where eighteen-wheelers were passing on highways below us. It has been a fantastic experience!

One would likely suspect that, with this breadth of flight adventures, we would have logged several memorable experiences. Indeed we have! And fortunately, most of them were pleasant. As one notable example, the most delightful sunset I have likely ever beheld is the one I witnessed while taking off from Oceano

County Airport and climbing out over the Pacific shoreline. Oceano is located adjacent to the Pacific Coast in California between San Luis Obispo to the north and Vandenberg Air Force Base to the south, and the takeoff runway is virtually due west out over the coastline. The sun had just slipped below the horizon prior to our climb-out, leaving its orange glow right at the water's edge. The air was warm and still. As we climbed straight out over the ocean, the scene that spread out before us was a glorious depiction of all that was right with the world. It was sufficiently breathtaking that I momentarily forgot to turn back toward land. I've seen many outstanding sunsets in a lifetime, but there was something special about this one; suspended in space, we were more than witnessing this spectacular scene – we were part of it.

In the grand scheme of scenic flights that one might ever experience through general aviation, I would venture to say that flying over the American Southwest would rate among the best. The southwestern deserts present vistas that are unique in the world. The jutting buttes, the wind-carved cliffs of multicolored sandstone, the towering mesas, and the myriad of wandering arroyos and canyons carved by the occasional passing flash flood all combine in a timeless beauty frozen for all eternity in magnificent grandeur. It's a scene that's best experienced viscerally, to be taken in holistically, to become completely mesmerized by.

To a person only casually familiar with what would meet the criteria of a desert environment, the entire southwestern portion of the country might likely qualify in such a person's mind. After all, it's all arid with sparse vegetation, so what's the difference? But to those of us who actually live in this part of the world, a distinction indeed exists. In reality, there are four discrete deserts comprising this region, plus a high plateau section – the Colorado Plateau encompassing northern Arizona and southern Utah – that receives too much rainfall to qualify as a true desert. The higher elevations of the Colorado Plateau may get upward of twenty inches of rainfall annually. That's considerable when compared with the Mojave Desert's annual rainfall of five inches. But to a person from Houston, where as much as fifty inches per year is experienced, the Colorado Plateau – the expanse that completely envelops the Grand Canyon and the Four Corners region – is still a desert.

Of the four deserts, the Great Basin, which spans from the eastern edge of California and covers virtually all of Nevada while also taking in western Utah and southeastern Idaho, is the coldest in that it receives a considerable amount of snow in the winter. Of the remaining three, the Mojave Desert would likely qualify as the hottest, as it also is the home of Death Valley. But it's in the Sonoran Desert of southern Arizona and northern Mexico, where the prominent saguaro cacti grow as high as forty feet tall with their upstretched arms reaching to the sky. And one finds oneself in the Chihuahuan Desert upon entering southern New Mexico and west Texas. Each of these regions is surprisingly unique with different flora, discrete geology, and diverse temperature extremes.

We have flown over these southwest deserts to various destinations countless times. The scenes are outstanding, especially in the late afternoon when the shadows are long and the colors are enhanced by the afternoon sun. There's a stark beauty of the desert, devoid of vegetation – defined by what isn't there. These deserts remain relatively unpopulated, and save for the occasional highway, the features have endured fairly unchanged over the centuries. Many of these numerous flights we have taken have been to visit friends in both Denver and Albuquerque, and the routes we selected would steer us over breathtaking scenic terrain.

When flying to Denver, we would typically make it a two-day trip with a fuel stop in either Kingman or at Prescott's Love Airport, both in Arizona. Our destination for the day would be

Farmington, New Mexico, in the Four Corners region, which gave us a well-positioned starting point for crossing the Rockies the next morning. If the fuel-stop choice were Prescott, we would typically leave Love Airport on a northeasterly heading toward Winslow, where we found it to be great fun to fly over the Meteor Crater, found south of the Painted Desert.

The Meteor Crater, which is located a few miles west of our navigational aid at Winslow, is an impact crater of approximately three quarters of a mile in diameter and 560 feet deep. Some fifty thousand years ago, a large nickel-iron meteorite slammed into the terrain at an estimated thirty thousand miles per hour, splashing tons of dirt up onto the surface. Because of the arid environment, even after all this time it remains as one of Earth's better preserved impact craters.

From there we would continue northeast across the picturesque Chuska Mountains, where we would pass by peaks that were well over nine thousand feet high. On the eastern side of this range, we would begin our descent into the Four Corners Regional Airport at Farmington, past a lone prominent outcropping to our north, Shiprock Peak.

When we would depart out of Kingman, we would take the route immediately outside of the restricted zone along the southern rim of the Grand Canyon. We would cross the Grand Canyon National Park Airport, follow the airway to Tuba City, and then fly across the Black Mesa and on to Farmington. That was a more scenic route, but it would take us a bit longer.

Black Mesa is approximately twenty nautical miles south of Monument Valley, another extremely scenic region that we have flown over. Located entirely within the Navajo Reservation on the Arizona-Utah border, Monument Valley's incredible red sandstone buttes and mesas rising hundreds of feet into the air epitomize virtually everyone's image of the American Southwest.

The credit for this depiction goes to John Ford, the movie director who selected this location for his many films starring John Wayne. The epic Westerns *Stagecoach* and *Fort Apache* filmed there immediately come to mind.

For the times we flew to Albuquerque, we would make the total trip in one day with our fuel stop and pilot exchange at Prescott. The flight time from Prescott to Albuquerque was about two and a half hours. If we arrived at Prescott Love Airport around noon, we typically would expect to be in Albuquerque by four o'clock with the one-hour time change. We would depart Prescott on a northeasterly heading toward the Zuni VOR and start climbing. The Mogollon Plateau a few miles east of Prescott has several peaks in the neighborhood of eight thousand feet, so we typically climbed to ninety-five hundred feet. Also, that altitude was acceptable for the high plateau directly east of Zuni, if we stayed on the airway. However, we would occasionally lose radio contact with air traffic control as the terrain rose up. In our early years of flying when we went to Albuquerque, we would climb to 11,500 feet to avoid this communication difficulty. But as we became more familiar with the route itself, we found that this radio-loss hiccup was only a mild inconvenience for not having to expend the additional fuel for the climb. And besides, flying closer to the ground gave us a more imposing view of the surrounding scenery. The canyons and mesas south of Gallup that we would pass over presented a stunning sight when the afternoon sun's rays were bringing out the colors and showing the enhanced chiseled features of the canyon walls.

The city of Albuquerque is located along the Rio Grande River in a valley that the river has helped cut over eons. And the high plateau drops off fairly abruptly into this valley some fifty or so miles west of the city. On the majority of our trips we would fly directly into Albuquerque International Airport, as it is configured with four separate runways where one can land from virtually any direction depending upon the winds – and the winds can be quite unpredictable. And over the years we have landed on or taken off from almost all of them. In addition, one of the general-aviation fixed-base operators, or FBOs, that we would frequent was very receptive to the needs of our class of airplane. If we were merely using Albuquerque as a fuel stop, however, we would fly into the Double Eagle airport, located on the west side of the river. It was easier for general aviation to get in and get out than was the international airport.

In the summer we would quite often be faced with the buildup of distant thunderheads as we descended into the valley west of the Rio Grande. The billows would start over the Sandia Mountains east of the city and expand into the valley itself. The late afternoon sun would render them as seemingly solid golden dollops of whipped cream with fluff oozing out from all over. Watching this scene unfold from high above the ground was an otherworldly experience. And by early evening, rain and lightning would follow.

We have flown into Mexico numerous times, and each flight seemed to offer some especially memorable experience, each bringing its own unique adventure. Since our airplane was based at the El Monte Airport in Southern California, we typically chose to clear Mexican customs in Mexicali. Its location immediately south of the US border but away from the bustle of Tijuana made it more convenient for general aviation. However, there always seemed to be several stations we had to go through in the customs-clearing process, such as getting our visas, paying any fees, and so forth that culminated in filing a Mexican flight plan, which was required for all flights in Mexico.

At the time we were making these trips, the world of aviation in Mexico was heavily male dominated, as it was considered to be a bit macho to fly airplanes. Hence, the section of the flight plan, which was in Spanish, asking for the pilot's name was labeled *el piloto,* in the masculine gender. With our limited command of Spanish, we were never able to come across where a feminine equivalent, such as *la pilota*, was ever used or even existed. We found this to be a bit amusing. So to interject a bit of humor – or confusion – into the Mexican flight traffic control system, under *el piloto* we would often write "La Senora Penny Moynihan." We often wondered if the controllers ever realized that a mere woman was the pilot in command of an airplane!

At one of the processing stations we always had to clear before filing our flight plan, we were required to fill out paperwork indicating that we were importing an airplane into Mexico. This was done on a letter-size form with all the aircraft details identified. When completed, we were handed the pink copy. Mexican law requires that we keep this copy with the aircraft at all times and then turn it in when clearing Mexican customs upon our return to the United States. This little pink sheet played an important and somewhat amusing role on one of our trips.

In the early afternoon of July 11, 1991, there was to be a total eclipse of the sun that would be visible from the lower tip of Baja California, south of La Paz, before it continued on to western Mexico and Central America. Prior to this event, our friends and fellow pilots, Gordon and Shirley Hughes, had recently joined Club Las Cruces, a private club that had its own secluded runway near its location. When they heard about the eclipse essentially passing directly overhead their new getaway, they invited us to join them at this facility to spend a couple of days and experience a first-hand view of the disappearing sun. We immediately accepted, and the four of us began laying out our plans. Because we knew that air traffic to this event would be extremely heavy, we decided that we would make our first stop in the town of Mulege, where we would spend the first night. Mulege is located on the eastern shoreline about halfway down the Baja California peninsula. We felt that by staying there, we would have covered the majority of the distance to our destination, yet be far enough north so as not to be seriously impacted by the heavier air traffic. The remaining leg of the trip would be fairly short.

We departed for Mulege the day before the eclipse, cleared Mexican customs at Mexicali, and continued on to the landing strip adjacent the Mulege Hotel Serenidad. Our original goal was to stay that first night at the Hotel Serenidad itself, and the reason for that choice was twofold. First, we had stayed at that hotel in the past and liked it, but most importantly it operated the general-aviation landing strip for the town. Although it was a compacted dirt runway, at that time it was very well maintained.

When we arrived at the Hotel Serenidad landing strip, we parked our two planes together at the runway edge adjacent to the wall leading into the Serenidad lobby. However, because of the very heavy demand for hotel rooms due to the eclipse, we were unable to book into the Hotel Serenidad itself. Using the phone in the Serenidad lobby, we found rooms available in a motel across the Rio de Santa Rosalia river in the main part of the town. We returned to our planes to unload our luggage for the night and then hailed a cab to take us across the river to our motel. Once there, we settled in for a relaxing afternoon as we prepared for our continued leg the next morning to the private resort south of La Paz.

Because of the limited airplane parking spaces available off the private runway at our ultimate destination, we decided that all four of us would fly the final leg in Gordon's Mooney, leaving our plane parked at Hotel Serenidad. To accommodate this schedule, we booked our Mulege hotel for two more nights – the night when we would be at the resort and the following night when we returned north. This allowed us to leave any surplus luggage behind, which we did to lighten Gordon's plane.

After breakfast at our hotel the morning of the eclipse, we once more got a cab to take us to the Hotel Serenidad, where we all climbed into Gordon's Mooney. Each couple brought only a small overnight bag with toiletries and a change of clothes. The flight took a little over an hour. We landed in the late morning, parked, and checked into our rooms. We then went outside and scouted out an ideal observation point where we would have an unobstructed view of the upcoming eclipse. There was not a cloud in the sky, and the sun would be completely covered sometime in the early afternoon.

And what an eclipse it was! We were fortunate that this eclipse occurred during a period of increasing solar activity. Once the moon had totally covered the sun, the pronounced solar flares occurring along the sun's corona became dramatically obvious. One flare was so extensive it seemed to be nearly 10 percent of the diameter of the sun. Several other people who were eclipse followers gathered where we were, and they happily filled us in with all the details of this unfolding event. It was a glorious experience. At the point where the sun was completely covered by the moon and the eclipse was total, the more prominent stars became visible, and the birds had become still as if they had gone to roost. This setting seemed suspended for a much greater duration than the few minutes it took for the moon to pass. But as the moon passed, we watched the events that had preceded the eclipse unfold in reverse – the dancing diffraction shadows, initially very pronounced, began to fade; the deep half-moon patterns formed from the shadows cast by sunbeams through the leaves grew to normal shapes; and the sounds of the birds' singing began to reappear.

When the eclipse was completed and our astronomical world had returned to normal, we had a tour of the resort facilities and generally hung out until dinner. This resort seemed to cater virtually exclusively to well-to-do *gringo* clientele, as the trappings were elegant and very well appointed.

We had planned for a casual departure the following day since we were only going as far north as Mulege, where we would spend one more night. Hence, we arose fairly late that morning and had a leisurely breakfast. Since the majority of the people who were at the resort had flown in for the eclipse, we felt that our delaying tactic would allow time for most of the parked aircraft to clear the area. And our plan worked. It was noonish by the time we clambered back into Gordon's plane and took off for Mulege.

Our arrival back at the Hotel Serenidad runway was completely uneventful. Someone had taken Gordon's original parking space next to our Mooney, so Gordon pulled off the runway on the opposite side and parked nose forward with the tail pointing toward our plane across the way.

As he shut down the engine and we started to gather our stuff to depart the aircraft, a young *federale* approached the plane and hailed us. The *federales* are the de facto state police in Mexico. Shirley opened the airplane door and inquired as to what he wanted. He asked us for something in Spanish, but we didn't immediately understand him. Realizing that he didn't know English, Shirley asked him again but this time in Spanish. He wanted to inspect the pink form validating the legal import of an airplane into Mexico. Shirley told him there was no problem and turned inside to rummage through her purse, looking for the pink sheet for their plane. Then she said, without turning back to the young *federale*, "Oh my God! I left it in the motel room with all of our other stuff! What are we going to tell him?"

It suddenly occurred to me from the back seat that this may not be a problem. I told Shirley to hold on for a second, as Penny had the pink sheet for *our* airplane in her purse. While Penny was retrieving the form, I suggested that all he was likely interested in was the existence of *a* pink sheet legitimizing the airplane import. He would not necessarily look closely at the scribbled carbon imprints with the specific airplane identifications. Penny handed the sheet to Shirley, who in turn handed it to the *federale*. He glanced at it quickly and handed it back. He smiled, thanked us, and walked away. We all sat there for a second and then had a brief chuckle – not at him, but at the situation. His verifying that the plane parked directly behind us was legally imported saved us a major inconvenience of a round-trip cab ride to the hotel to retrieve the correct paperwork!

Our many flights into Mexico have also rewarded us with numerous unique experiences with negotiating different variations of unpaved runways, many of which were less than optimal. Two examples immediately come to mind. The first instance, also involving our friends Gordon and Shirley, was a flight from Loreto, Mexico, to Mexicali, where we landed at Punta Final for a couple of hours. Punta Final is a quaint Mexican village adjacent the Sea of Cortez on the eastern coast of Baja California and is located about two thirds of the way from Loreto en route to Mexicali. The runway at Punta Final was fairly short, barely over twenty-nine hundred feet. And it was fairly soft. Landing there was no problem, except that we noticed that our tires were sinking a little farther into the surface than we had expected.

Taking off from there, however, was a different story. The runway was nearly perpendicular to the coastline, and because of higher terrain south and east of it, the departure direction was northeast directly over the coast. But there was a berm that ran along the coast that, from the ground, looked to be a lot higher than it likely was, and there were buildings atop it. I estimated that this combination represented a barrier height of at least twenty feet that we had to clear, and it was positioned fairly close to the end of the runway. When we returned to our airplanes, we noticed that the entire runway was quite sandy, and our tires were already sunk into it by a good three inches. The four of us discussed our takeoff plans and noted that this single departure would require combining all three of the special takeoff techniques everyone had practiced in primary training – a soft-field takeoff, a short-field takeoff, and a steep climb-out to clear an obstruction.

Everyone collectively decided that Penny and I would leave first, and I would be in the left seat for the departure. I started the engine and taxied to the extreme departure end of the runway. I set the controls to half flaps and, with the brakes on, brought the engine to its maximum RPM. Then I released the brakes. The plane jerked slightly while the wheels got out of their ruts and then started forward. As the speed built up slightly, I was able to pop the plane upward out of the ruts and into the boundary layer, that layer of air that flows under the plane prior to takeoff. Then I had to push the nose down to keep the airplane in level flight while in the boundary layer, as we didn't yet have sufficient speed to generate the required lift for actual takeoff. We did, however, have adequate air compression under the wings to keep the wheels out of the soft surface, and by maintaining that condition, the airplane could then accelerate to takeoff speed. Once we reached that speed, I raised the nose, retracted the landing gear, and set the controls to the maximum climb angle, and we cleared the top of the berm by a good hundred feet. That was our first experience with an actual soft-field takeoff.

The second example of our unique Mexican runway experiences was our landing on the runway at Meling Ranch, a family-owned resort located some sixty miles due west of San

Felipe and near the west side of the San Pedro Martir mountains. This flight again involved two Mooneys with our friends Gordon and Shirley, and this time we had two passengers in ours – Fred and Chrik. We again stopped for fuel and customs in Mexicali before continuing onward. Because of a communications error, the fuel attendant added about fifteen gallons more fuel than we had requested, which would have been too much when combined with the passenger load we would be carrying. To take a little weight off, we changed passengers with Gordon. Chrik would ride with him and Shirley would ride with us. The weight difference was about a hundred pounds, bringing our total load back in line. We then took off for Meling Ranch.

The Meling Ranch runway is privately owned and operated, and the owners do a fairly good job maintaining it. Its surface is compacted dirt with crushed gravel, and like Punta Final its length is barely over twenty-nine hundred feet. The difference here, however, is that one can land in only one direction. But in that direction the runway is on a fairly significant uphill slope that dead-ends at a hill, giving one the illusion of landing into a box canyon. There is no go-around option. All parking was off the very end of the runway at the foot of the hill.

As we approached Meling Ranch, the visibility had become a bit hazy. To compensate for the reduced visibility, I wanted to ensure that we had a fairly long final approach leg to complete the landing setup with sufficient time that I could concentrate on where the wheels would touch down. As we neared the threshold, I noted two factors about the runway. First, I could see that the uphill slope was fairly significant. A normal landing speed would bring us to a stop midway up the runway, and we would have to add more than the usual amount of power in order to taxi to the end, where we would park. Second, there seemed to be an excessive amount of gravel on the runway, which meant that my adding power would suck up a lot of stones that could result in propeller damage. So I decided to approach the threshold a little faster than normal so that momentum would carry us a bit farther uphill, and maybe I wouldn't need to add as much power to taxi to parking. Shirley was a bit nervous about that decision, and rightfully so. There was, after all, an actual wall at the end of the runway in the form of a hill. From the back seat, things looked different, and she was concerned that I was coming in too fast. But from the front seat everything looked good, and all worked out fine. The plane slowed to a near stop about three fourths of the distance along the runway, and I still had to add a little extra power to taxi the plane to parking. However, this was the first time I had ever landed uphill into a box canyon on a dirt runway.

We had another landing experience in Mexico that's worth mentioning, but this time it was more benign and on a paved runway. We were beginning our return leg home from spending a few days in Puerto Vallarta and decided to stop by San Blas for an overnight stay. We were again a flight of two Mooneys with Gordon and Shirley, but this time we also had Fred and Jackie as passengers – Fred was with us and Jackie was with them. Gordon was in the left seat of their plane and I was there in ours. Gordon was in front of us. The hop from Puerto Vallarta to San Blas was fairly short, taking barely an hour, and we were flying relatively low. The vegetation in that region of Mexico is quite thick, and we were following the shoreline while passing over the jungle canopy. The scene below us was of some remote tropical wilderness, devoid of any apparent human influence or habitation. As we looked down at the tops of the palms, for a few moments at least we could have easily imagined that we were somewhere over central Brazil.

Whenever we flew with Gordon and Shirley as a flight of two, we always selected an unassigned radio frequency that we would use to communicate between our two airplanes. And we were frequently on the radio with each other throughout this flight. When Gordon arrived at San Blas, he told us that there were kids playing soccer on the runway. We learned later that this was fairly common, as that particular runway gets very little use. He said that he would first make a low pass over the runway to alert the kids that an airplane was about to land. He did that, and the kids scattered temporarily. He then circled around to land. Because the kids were still in the area, we told him over the radio that to be on the safe side we had better do the same also. As we started our low pass, Gordon was already landed and we could see that the kids were indeed starting to come back. So we buzzed the runway and turned to a left downwind to set up to land. Again the kids scattered. By the time we were on our final approach, the coast was clear and we landed without incident. We pulled in to park alongside Gordon. This was the first time that we have ever had to shoo kids off an active runway before landing.

As a noteworthy epilogue to this story, while we were getting out of the plane, a young *federale* approached us from the airport entrance gate, wanting to see our pink sheet showing that we had imported an aircraft. Since we always carry it with us, Penny had it in her purse and gave it to him. He glanced at it, smiled at us, and handed it back. Again, it likely could have been for any airplane.

In contrast with the fairly complex steps required for the border crossing into Mexico, the other extreme we experienced was crossing the border into Canada. In 2001 Penny and I were joined by another flying couple, Virginia and Dennis, as a flight of two to attend the Calgary Stampede, a major rodeo function put on every summer in Calgary, Canada. When charting our course prior to departure, we decided that the most direct route for us would be to fly to Cut Bank, Montana, which is south of

Calgary, and clear Canadian customs at Lethbridge, Alberta, a Canadian port of entry. Because of the long flight scheduled for the day we departed, we stayed the night in Cut Bank, with plans to do the border crossing first thing in the morning.

One part of the border-crossing procedure for Canada is to call their customs office prior to arriving and tell them who is coming, the type of aircraft, its tail or N number, and the approximate time of arrival. After breakfast that morning, I volunteered to make this call and give the customs officials everyone's information. We then headed out to the Cut Bank Airport, did our preflight inspections, and filed our border-crossing flight plan – a requirement of the US side. We then piled into our respective airplanes and headed off to Lethbridge.

Although it's an official port of entry for Canada, Lethbridge has a small general-aviation airport. When we arrived there, it was obvious where we needed to taxi to in order to clear customs, and both of our planes taxied into the customs area. We shut down our engines and climbed out of our planes. I then went to look for the customs agent, but there was no one around. I then noticed a telephone mounted near the corner of the fairly small adjacent building, and there was a relatively large sign to the left of the phone. I walked over to it, and the sign indicated a number to call for customs. Since this was a small airport, I assumed that the presence of the telephone meant that a customs agent is not on the premises all the time. If one is needed, then a phone call would bring him out. I picked up the phone receiver and dialed the number indicated. When the voice on the other end answered, I gave my name and the tail numbers of both airplanes and said that we were now at the customs ramp in Lethbridge. The voice then said "Thank you, and welcome to Canada!" Expecting something else, I then asked "Is that it?" The voice said, "Yup, and have a nice day." I hung up, turned to the rest of our party, and told them that we had been cleared and could continue on our way. We all got back into our airplanes and continued onward to Springbank, a general-aviation airport west of Calgary where we parked our planes for the duration of our stay. Our entire time in Lethbridge from landing to takeoff likely didn't last more than fifteen minutes. We were impressed.

And of course, no one's flying career is complete without at least once having landed and taken off from the highest public-use airport in North America, the Leadville Lake County airport. Located about two miles southwest of the town of Leadville, Colorado, and perched in a local mountain "valley" at an elevation of 9,934 feet, Leadville Lake County airport would offer a unique flight challenge on that warm July day.

One year on a Fourth of July weekend, six of us in a flight of three airplanes had decided to visit Taos, New Mexico, for a few days. While there, we all thought it would be fun to fly around the area and explore it from above. And one of our primary goals for this little adventure was to accept the challenge of landing at the Leadville Airport, and once there to visit the town itself.

The challenge that was presented to us can be summed up in the definition of the aviation parameter called density altitude. Basically, *density altitude* is defined as the altitude determined by the atmospheric pressure at one's elevation where that pressure altitude is corrected for nonstandard temperature. Stated more simply, density altitude is the altitude at which the airplane "thinks" it is flying. The Leadville Airport presents an excellent example of this. First, the standard temperature at Leadville's elevation is approximately 23°F, a temperature of nine degrees below freezing. But on that day in early July when we arrived, the temperatures were fairly warm, somewhere in the low seventies. When corrected for the actual temperature reading, the density altitude – the altitude at which the airplane thought it was flying that day – was approximately thirteen thousand feet.

The nonflying public may not fully appreciate the significance of the challenge we were subjecting ourselves to. Pilots use density altitude to assess the aerodynamic performance of their aircraft, to determine how well – or how poorly – it will perform. Everyone knows that the atmosphere becomes less dense the higher one climbs in altitude. And as the air becomes less dense, the air-fuel mixture ratio changes and causes the engine not to perform as well. But most airplanes have a manual adjustment that pilots routinely use to correct for that occurrence. However, a lowering of air density also reduces the lift generated by the wings, and pilots don't have direct control over that. Its influence is most obvious on landings and takeoffs – especially takeoffs. We discussed all these factors prior to our departure from Taos that morning.

After breakfast, the six of us headed off to our respective airplanes parked at the Taos Regional Airport – Gordon and Shirley Hughes to their Mooney, Dave and Colleen Campbell to their Piper Arrow, and Penny and I to our Mooney. The weather was clear with occasional high stratus clouds. I should note that the Taos Regional Airport itself is located at a respectable elevation of 7,095 feet and subject to similar density-altitude concerns.

We departed Taos on a north-northwest heading, climbed to 10,500 feet, and navigated via Alamosa following the valley formed by the Rockies on both sides. Leadville is on the order of two hundred miles from Taos in that direction on a fairly straight line, and our flight time would be approximately an hour and a half. The valley was predominantly farmland, with the fields irrigated by very large circular watering systems that would slowly crawl around a fixed center point, rendering hundreds of green circles on the landscape below. We joked with each other over the radio that these were crop circles left by visiting aliens.

The approach to Leadville was like that to any other airport, except for the eleven-thousand-foot pattern altitude. Landing conditions were favoring Runway 16 from the southerly direction, and landing via a right pattern was recommended. Since we were arriving from the south, we would enter the pattern on the right downwind leg for the assigned runway. Because of the very high density altitude, as well as actual altitude, another factor that pilots must pay close attention to is landing airspeed. The pilot must adhere to what his indicated airspeed says on his airspeed gauge and not concentrate on how fast the terrain seems to be passing by. The indicated airspeed will be slower than what he would normally associate with the rate of the terrain he sees passing below him. But the indicated airspeed is based on the ram speed of the thinner air entering the pitot tube and hence is reflecting the reduced density. And reduced density means lower lift on the wings, necessitating a higher actual speed. But all of this is second nature to the seasoned pilot, and all three airplanes touched down without incident.

After parking our planes, we arranged with the local FBO for a shuttle into the town of Leadville itself. As we started exploring the town, we were surprised to learn of its amazingly colorful history. We knew it was once a silver-mining town, but we didn't know that the silver discovery resulted from frustrations with placer mining of gold. A heavy black sand kept impeding the miners' sluice boxes until someone identified the sand as cerussite, or lead carbonate, which typically is also high in silver. When traced to its source, several lead-silver deposits were discovered, thus starting the silver boom in the late 1870s. At the beginning of the silver boom, Leadville, originally named Silver City, became one of the West's most lawless towns. Gunfighters and gamblers poured in. One of the town founders and early mayors, Horace Tabor, was concerned about the lawlessness and hired one of Denver's most notorious gunfighters, Mart Duggan, to subdue the violence and restore order, which Duggan successfully accomplished.[12] Tabor later went on to become a US senator. And there is some speculation that the name Matt Dillon from the TV series *Gunsmoke* may have been derived from Mart Duggan.

The town attracted people like Doc Holliday, who moved there shortly after the famous O.K. Corral incident. Shortly after arriving, he shot and wounded Billy Allen, who had demanded repayment of a five-dollar debt Doc owed him. Claiming self-defense despite overwhelming evidence to the contrary, he was found not guilty.

The patriarch of the Guggenheim family, Meyer Guggenheim, invested in the Leadville silver mines and went on to build one of the largest fortunes in the world at the time. The Guggenheim family later became well known for their philanthropy. As a specific example, in 1926 Meyer's son Daniel and grandson Harry, who was also an aviator, established the Daniel Guggenheim Fund for the Promotion of Aeronautics and created the Guggenheim Aeronautical Laboratory at the California Institute of Technology, which came to be known as GALCIT. This connection was of special interest to me because, up to the outbreak of World War II, GALCIT was the only university-based facility doing research on rocket engines and had developed the jet-assisted takeoff, or JATO, augmentation for aircraft. The advent of JATO led to the establishment of the Jet Propulsion Laboratory, from where I had recently retired after thirty-eight years.

The Guggenheim family was not unique in tracing their origins of international fame to Leadville. The socialite and philanthropist Margaret Brown had a similar beginning. The family of Margaret Brown became very wealthy through the

---

[12] Wikipedia. "Leadville," last modified July 29, 2019. https://en.wikipedia.org/wiki/Leadville,_Colorado.

discovery of a large gold ore seam. Margaret, whom everyone called Molly, became famous as a survivor of the *Titanic* sinking. She took command of one of the lifeboats and forced it to return and look for survivors, drafting the women aboard to help row. From this episode she became known as the unsinkable Molly Brown.

Horace Tabor also founded the Tabor Opera House, which is one of the most costly structures ever built in Colorado. All construction materials had to be brought in on wagons. Oscar Wilde gave a presentation from its stage to a packed house. Not to be outdone, the six of us also toured the opera house, even to the point of going out onto the stage. And while up there on stage, we all locked arms and did a simulated chorus-line dance.

Leadville, today a town of fewer than three thousand people, was once the second-largest city in Colorado, bested only by Denver, and was the first city proposed as the state capital, again beaten by Denver. Maybe this is but another example of nature's many cruel ironies; the glories of today are often forgotten tomorrow.

As the hour approached late afternoon, we all thought we should be heading to the airport for our flight back to Taos, so we arranged for a shuttle to pick us up. Once at the airport, the subject of needed fuel came up. We with the two Mooneys were okay for the hour-and-a-half trip back, but Dave indicated that their Piper Arrow may be marginal. As we discussed this issue further, the two women who ran the FBO joined in. One of them, who was a local flight instructor, recommended against adding fuel at Leadville unless the airplane was essentially on empty, which it was not. She recommended that they take off with their minimum fuel load but land at one of the nearby airports at a lower elevation and refuel there. She reiterated that it was a warm day by Leadville standards, and the density altitude was much higher than indicated by the airport elevation. There were several airports between Leadville and Taos where they could land and refuel. That was the option that Dave and Colleen chose, and they thanked her for her suggestion.

It was Penny's turn to be the official pilot in command in the left seat for our flight back, so I was in the right seat setting the turbocharger while she was doing the engine run-up. Our turbocharger was a Ray Jay retrofit, not standard issue for our model of Mooney. As a result, it functioned somewhat like having a second throttle. It had its own separate control knob to engage it, and I adjusted it to a manifold pressure appropriate for our altitude. We were ready to go. Penny announced our intentions and took the active runway, which was still the southbound Runway 16. With full throttle in, we headed down the sixty-four-hundred-foot runway and were nearly two thirds of the way along it before the wheels finally left the asphalt. The engine performed nicely, but it took a lot more actual speed before the wings realized that there was air flowing over their tops. But we were off with no problem. And very shortly, the land began to fall away as we left the Leadville plateau and the valley loomed before us. We set our heading for the Alamosa VOR, dropped our altitude to ninety-five hundred feet, and settled back for the cruise. It had been a great day.

Then there was the time we passed fairly close to George Washington's right lapel on Mount Rushmore as we descended for landing at the Rapid City, South Dakota, airport. The year was 1991, and the six of us had planned a Fourth of July trip to Mount Rushmore that year – Penny and I in our Mooney, Gordon and Shirley in theirs, and Fred and Jackie as our passengers. Since Mount Rushmore was dedicated in 1941 and would be celebrating its fiftieth anniversary, we all thought it would be special to visit there during the celebration year. And the Fourth of July would be an ideal time for us to go.

Since the Fourth fell on a Thursday, both Penny and I got Thursday and Friday off from work as paid holidays. In order to expand our total trip time, we also took Tuesday and Wednesday as vacation days, making Monday our last workday that week. With Gordon and Shirley living in the San Jose area at that time, our plan was to fly to San Jose with Fred and Jackie on Tuesday, where all of us would spend that night with Gordon and Shirley. We would then leave from San Jose on Wednesday morning for Rapid City, South Dakota, with one additional person in each of our airplanes. Jackie would go with Gordon and Shirley and Fred with us.

With our plans now crystalized, Fred and Jackie showed up at our house fairly early Tuesday morning. We loaded everyone and the overnight bags into our car and headed out. Since we had planned that we would have four people plus baggage in the plane for that leg of the trip, we had already reduced our fuel load accordingly. It was only a two-and-a-half-hour flight, so we still had plenty of reserve. Although the sky conditions were mostly clear when we took off, there was a general haze throughout the valley, so we filed for an IFR flight anyway. Flying IFR removed any airspace clearance issues that might arise during our departure and arrival stages and would give us priority into San Jose.

After an uneventful flight – the best kind, by the way – we landed at San Jose and taxied to the general-aviation terminal for fuel and parking for the night. Gordon and Shirley were both waiting for us inside the general aviation, or GA, terminal. All six of us sardined into their car and left the terminal for their house located over the hill in Boulder Creek.

The next morning we were all back at the San Jose airport to officially begin our five-day vacation trip. Our plan for the first leg of the flight was to land at Winnemucca, Nevada, for a fuel stop and to change pilots. From Winnemucca we would continue on to Ogdon, Utah, where again we would make a fuel stop and pilot exchange. Having two pilots aboard each airplane is a considerable advantage in avoiding fatigue on long flights. The third leg of our flight took us all the way to Rapid City, South Dakota.

We were lucky with the weather, as the skies were clear and the temperatures were warm for the entire trip. We were able to fly under visual flight rules, or VFR, for all three legs. Because of the excellent visibility, we spotted the back side of Mount Rushmore from a considerable distance as we approached it from the west. We started our descent a bit early so as to get a closer look at the sculptures prior to our arrival into Rapid City. By the time we reached the mountain crest, we were barely five hundred feet above the south end of the artwork and still descending. It was late afternoon, and the shadows from the soft light cast across the carvings accentuated the facial features. George was to our left and slightly below us. We looked down at the bridge of his nose as we prepared to enter the pattern for landing at Rapid City.

Once on the ground, we got fuel and arranged for parking the airplanes for the next couple of days. We then checked out a rental car. Since there were six of us, we ended up with a large Suburban that was a few years old. We didn't care what the vehicle looked like; we just needed the room! While we were waiting for our rental car to arrive, we reserved our motel rooms. In the morning we planned to drive to the Mount Rushmore National Monument.

After a leisurely local breakfast, we all piled into the Suburban and headed out to Mount Rushmore. When we arrived, we were treated to a very impressive and informative information center, where we learned enriching details of the monument's evolution.

We all knew that the monument is located in the Black Hills of South Dakota and that the four presidents represented are Washington, Jefferson, Teddy Roosevelt, and Lincoln. But there were a myriad of other fascinating aspects about the monument that at least I was completely unaware of. For instance, I never knew that the original plan was to place Thomas Jefferson to Washington's right and that the carving for this placement had actually begun and continued for a year and a half. However, the granite at that location was comprised of too much quartz that the carvers kept blasting off. They finally decided that a carving of Jefferson was not going to work at that location and blasted off the entire face and relocated it. The repositioning of Jefferson to Washington's left seemed to nonetheless work out fine for Washington.

The original intent of Mount Rushmore was purely as a tourist attraction, conceived by Doane Robinson as a means of attracting people to South Dakota.[13] Robinson selected Gutzon Borglum as the sculptor, and work began in 1927. Fourteen years later, in 1941, the project was completed. Unfortunately, Borglum died seven months before he could see the finished product, and the remainder of the sculpting was overseen by his son. On October 31, 1941, the monument was dedicated, and we were there for its semicentennial.

When we returned to Rapid City, we were greeted by a Fourth of July flyover of the city's main street by a fighter squadron from nearby Ellsworth Air Force Base. Later that evening we watched a fireworks display from the second-story balcony of our motel. We dedicated the following day to exploring the local area and driving through Custer State Park looking for bison, of which we saw only one. And of course we had to include a visit to Deadwood, the

---

[13] Wikipedia. "Mount Rushmore," last modified August 1, 2019. https://en.wikipedia.org/wiki/Mount_Rushmore.

famous frontier town where Wild Bill Hickok met his untimely end while playing poker in a salon on Main Street. When he was shot, he was holding a pair of aces and a pair of eights, a hand that has since become known as the Deadman's Hand.

On Saturday it was time to begin our journey back home but not without more exploration, this time by air. After breakfast and checking out of our motel, we left for the airport and turned in the Suburban at the rental car desk. We had decided the night before that our destination for the day would be Cody, Wyoming, where we would spend the night. But there were several geological features that we wanted to see from the air along the way, and the first was the Badlands National Park. The Badlands is some sixty miles southeast of Rapid City, which by air means that it's only about twenty minutes away. We had good weather and great visibility that morning, so we took off from the airport under VFR and climbed to about fifty-five hundred feet. Again, Fred was with us while Jackie went with Gordon and Shirley.

The Badlands National Park presents a most impressive geology. The landscape is comprised of thousands of pale, weathered pinnacles flowing downward in irregular patterns of peaked lumps as if some Titan had spread massive amounts of partially hardened plaster over thousands of acres. There is no apparent contiguous canyon throughout the entire terrain; and there definitely was no place where we could have made an emergency landing, if such a need were to arise. The elevation of the park is around thirty-three hundred feet, and we weren't winging much above that.

After a few minutes of flying over the Badlands, we turned northwest and then north to put us on a heading for the Black Hills that would set us up nicely for a flyby of Mount Rushmore. Seeing the mountain sculptures from the ground is impressive on its own, but looking down on them as we flew over was a uniquely remarkable experience altogether.

We again were communicating with each other on our interplane common frequency. Our goal after the Mount Rushmore flyby was to find and fly by Devils Tower in northeastern Wyoming. We had an approximate idea of our desired heading, but we stayed in communication with each other to compare notes along the way. As Lincoln's face disappeared from view, we climbed to eighty-five hundred feet for terrain clearance, since many of the local peaks in the Black Hills easily reach seven thousand feet. We set the nose of the airplane on an estimated heading of three hundred degrees and watched for landmarks to make adjustments. Devils Tower is approximately eighty miles from Mount Rushmore.

Our dead-reckoning navigation was quite good, as we spotted Devils Tower slightly to our northwest when we arrived in the vicinity of where we thought it should be. In fact, it was fairly easy to spot. Devils Tower juts out of the surrounding prairie to stand by itself as a nearly one-thousand-foot-high, roughly cylindrical prominence of vertically striated rock. Several Devils Tower origin theories have been offered by geologists and local natives alike. Geologists think it possibly arose from the extrusion of harder igneous rock through sedimentary beds, or maybe we are seeing the remnants of a volcanic plug after the softer outer rock has eroded away. The tower's striations have spawned several folk tales from the local Native American tribes, and virtually all of them tell the story of how giant bears left the huge scratch marks pursuing children who had wandered from their village.[14] In Lakota culture it was a group of girls who, when playing, were chased by several giant bears and escaped to a large rock. They

---

[14] Wikipedia. "Devils Tower," last modified July 24, 2019. https://en.wikipedia.org/wiki/Devils_Tower.

prayed for help from the Great Spirit, who made the rock rise out of the ground with the girls atop it. The bears scrambled up its sides, but the walls were too steep. The striations resulted from the giant claw marks left by the struggling bears. The story from Sioux folklore involves two boys and a single bear, but the outcome is similar. But whatever its origin, the vertical hexagonal columns that form its striations are thought to be the result of cooling magma. Erosion of the softer sedimentary rock over the eons slowly exposed this lone monument.

As we got closer to the tower and while talking to each other on the radio, we decided that we couldn't pass up the opportunity to fly around it. So we descended to an altitude that put us a little above halfway of its height and turned to circle it. Since all of us had seen the movie *Close Encounters of the Third Kind* that had come out over a decade earlier, we were joking over the radio while flying around the tower about whether we were able to see evidence of the alien spacecraft.

Once we satisfied ourselves that all the aliens had departed Devils Tower, we turned due west toward Cody and started climbing. In less than an hour we would be crossing the Bighorn Mountains that peak around thirteen thousand feet, and our tower fly-about had left us below five thousand feet. We leveled off at 12,500 feet, which gave us about a thousand-foot clearance at the location where we crossed the Bighorns south of Sheridan, Wyoming.

Now on the west side of the Bighorn Mountains with great visibility and the sun getting low on the horizon, we started our descent into Cody. The Cody airport was uncontrolled, meaning that there was no active control tower. When approaching an uncontrolled airport, the onus is on the pilot to communicate with other air traffic that may be in the area to let them know where he is and what his intentions are. The pilot also states his position as he enters the traffic pattern and again as he enters the different pattern legs, such as turning to the base leg and turning to final. As it turned out, when we arrived at Cody, we were the only two airplanes in the vicinity. So we entered the pattern, landed, and taxied for fuel and overnight parking. Once we parked and took care of our airplanes, we arranged for our motel for the night and set out to explore Cody.

The following day was Sunday and time for us to head home directly. So the day would comprise flying for the majority of the time, with a couple of planned fuel stops. The weather was good to us again with clear skies, and we departed Cody southwest bound, climbing again to 12,500 feet to clear the mountains east of the Great Salt Lake. Our first fuel stop was at Provo, Utah, which took us nearly three hours from Cody. Fueled up and back in the air, our next stop was in St. George, Utah, near the Nevada border. South of Provo we started to see high clouds and encountered occasional turbulence, all of which were the remnants of a storm off the coast of Baja California.

It would be after our stop in St. George that our two airplanes would part ways. Gordon and Shirley would be heading on to San Jose, so Jackie, who had been flying with them, would now rejoin us in our plane for our final leg home. Because of the additional weight we would be carrying, we didn't take on as much fuel. But the flight time to El Monte would be only about two and a half hours, so again we still had plenty of margin. With fresh fuel on board each aircraft, we all said our goodbyes and headed southwest. Shortly after our departure we flew into a few more remnants of the Baja California storm, only this time they were scattered cumulus clouds at a lower altitude. Flying around and below them provided us with a bit of entertainment until we arrived at El Monte. Our wheels' touching down on Runway 19 marked the grand finale of a great trip.

These are but a few examples of how flight has extensively expanded our horizons and enabled experiences not possible from the ground. When traveling by car, one is fundamentally restricted to one-dimensional space. The automobile is confined to the road and can go either forward or backward along it, but no other option is possible. Flight, by contrast, is four dimensional – the three spatial dimensions and time. Roads are unnecessary. When we are flying, we can go up or down or sideways as we so choose. But unlike ground travel, time also becomes a critical parameter – the time to the destination, the time between fuel stops, the time for a procedure turn in instrument conditions, the time in a hold. Being in the sky is like being in a different universe.

To see these vast landscapes from high above the ground and with no surrounding walls is, in the words of Walt Whitman, like seeing the "world in a grain of sand, and a Heaven in a wild flower." It's a dreamlike experience that renews our perception of the natural beauty forever surrounding us and balances our assessment of the world. All of this becomes possible with wings.

Flight has enabled us to access extraordinary and faraway places in barely a weekend's time that would normally take days by other means. When in the air, we witness panoramas from perspectives unlike anything we have ever seen. A truly three-dimensional world presents itself during every airborne second. With wings we are unconstrained. With wings we are literally above the world, seeing things no one else has seen over ground where no one has ever walked. Wings are definitely a gift.

CHAPTER 3

GALS WHO TAKE PLANES IN THE AIR

I've never met a hardier bunch,
Or a group more devil-may-care
Than the gals who don their flying togs
And take airplanes into the air.

They're pretty, they're smart,
They're perky, they're proud.
They take every step with a flair.
Those gals who don their flying togs
And take airplanes into the air.

They know where they are,
And they know where they've been,
And go boldly where most never dare.

Those gals who don their flying togs
And take airplanes into the air.

They're leading the charge,
They're saving the world!
They've got grace and courage to spare.
They're the gals who don their flying togs
And take airplanes into the air.

Somewhere along the way while we were involved with our IFR training, Penny was contacted by one of the local women pilots about joining the Ninety-Nines, or 99s as their name is often written, an international organization composed solely of women pilots. Considering that barely 7 percent of licensed pilots are women, then, as the poem suggests, women pilots are a special class unique unto themselves. There are no shrinking violets in their ranks. And 100 percent of the Ninety-Nines are licensed pilots. I found them to be an impressive group of people with whom to associate.

The Ninety-Nines as an organization was founded on November 2, 1929, when twenty-six women met at the Curtiss Airport in Valley Stream, New York, in response to a letter sent to all licensed women pilots in the country. At the time the letter went out, there were only 117 women pilots nationwide, and of those, only eighty-six responded. And of those who did, only twenty-six actually made it to the Curtiss Airport. The objectives of this new organization were to assemble women pilots for mutual support, advance aviation, and create a central office to keep files on women in aviation. There was a struggle the first year to establish themselves and keep the group together, but during their group meeting in 1931, Amelia Earhart, likely the most famous of the original women pilots, was voted in as the group's first elected president. But prior to the organization's first formal election of its president, the group, under the leadership of acting president Opal Kunz, set about to select a name for the organization. Two of their members, Amelia Earhart and Jean Hoyt, proposed that the name be taken from the total sum of the original charter members. Since eighty-six women responded to the original letter, the name 86s was originally chosen. Then eleven more of the original 117 joined, and the name was changed to the 97s. With the later addition again of two others, the name was changed once more to the 99s. It was decided after the last change that the name would remain permanent.[15]

From its very inception, membership in the Ninety-Nines has been opened to all women who became licensed pilots. Today, the Ninety-Nines boasts fifty-one hundred members and is represented throughout forty-four countries, with its international headquarters in Oklahoma City. Their ranks are filled by professional airline pilots, military pilots, flight instructors, and women like Penny who merely fly for pleasure.

Penny was an active member of the San Gabriel Valley Chapter of the Ninety-Nines for well over a decade. She even served two terms as the chapter chairman. Because of her involvement in this organization, we had the opportunity to participate in numerous aviation-related events that they coordinated. Husbands and significant others were allowed to participate with the Ninety-Nines in these activities as "Forty-Nine and a Halves." Interestingly, not all Forty-Nine and a Halves were licensed pilots,

---

[15] Jorski, Jason. "History of Women Pilots. History of the 99s." 2011. Ninety Nines Museum of Women Pilots. https://web.archive.org/web/20140224020321/http://www.museumofwomenpilots.com/Histof99.html.

but those who weren't were good sports in supporting their wives' or friends' passion for flying.

In fact, the San Gabriel Valley Ninety-Nines recognized that many of their supporters were not pilots, and their chapter would periodically conduct a Flying Companion seminar. This seminar would typically be an all-day event where several of their members, along with an FAA-designated flight examiner, would give presentations on the fundamentals of flight. They would explain the principles of the four basic force vectors of lift, weight, thrust, and drag, typically spending a little more time showing how air flowing over the top of the airfoil creates lift. They would explain the importance of weight and balance, demonstrating to their nonflying friends that an airplane is like a teeter-totter balanced at the center of gravity – and define what the center of gravity is. They would talk about the importance of weather and what it means to pilots, as well as describe designations of the air spaces we fly through and the defined airways, the "highways in the sky" we use. All in all, theirs was an excellent primer course to help put their flying companions' minds at ease that airplanes don't fall out of the sky.

As an example of one of the aviation events, every year as a fundraiser their chapter would coordinate a poker run that would often begin at the Brackett Airport in Pomona, California, and would involve pilot participants buying one or more poker hands. They would then fly to four different preassigned airports, at each of which they would receive an envelope containing one card for each hand they had bought. The envelopes would be marked with a symbol, such as a plus sign, a square, or a star, for each hand they had. They would return to Brackett as their final airport, where they would receive their fifth envelope. The participants would then submit their envelopes to a Ninety-Nine volunteer, who would open them and judge the hands. Prizes that had been donated by various sponsors would be awarded based on the best hands. When the awards were concluded, everyone would be welcomed to a barbecue.

Meanwhile, chapter members who handed out the envelopes to the participants would fly or drive to the preassigned airports and set up in positions that would be obvious to the poker players who would fly in. That was the role we typically filled. And since we had one of the faster airplanes, we usually volunteered for the farthest airport. The barbecue would typically be well underway by the time we arrived back at Brackett. During the early morning on at least two occasions, we had to fly in to our assigned airport under IFR conditions because the airport was overcast. Since the poker run was a VFR event, the overcast did not dissipate sufficiently during the day in either of these two cases for all participants to land and get their cards. So we gave our leftover cards to the Ninety-Nines volunteer when we returned, and she filled out the missing hands.

Money raised by the poker run and other similar events is collected by the chapter and allotted to the chapter's various aviation scholarships. For example, scholarship funds have been set up in the memory of each of two fellow San Gabriel Valley Ninety-Nines whom we have lost. One is the Linda Hayden Memorial Future Woman Pilot Scholarship, a thousand-dollar scholarship created in honor of Linda Hayden to be awarded to a deserving student pilot. The other is the Jean Bustos Perpetual Scholarship, a thousand-dollar scholarship specifically awarded to a mature woman pilot seeking further advancement in her aviation interests that can be spent where needed.

The San Gabriel Valley Ninety-Nines were also actively involved with the annual competitions sponsored by the Pacific Coast Intercollegiate Flying Association, or PCIFA. The PCIFA would sponsor regional Safety and Flight Evaluation Conferences

(SAFECONs) that would rotate among a half dozen aviation schools, and flight students from all of these schools would participate. Students would typically compete in five academic events and five flying events during this competition. The Ninety-Nines would provide the army of judges required for such functions as judging power-on and power-off landings, message drops, instrument flights, and navigation events, and the ranks of this army would be made up heavily from drafted Forty-Nine and a Halves, including me.

One of the truly fun annual events Penny's chapter participated in was the Southwest Section meetings. These meetings were three-day events that involved all the Ninety-Nines chapters in the five states of the Pacific Southwest – California, Hawaii, Arizona, Nevada, and Utah. Typically one of the chapters would be the host sponsor. There would be a myriad of aviation-related interests presented during these meetings, ranging from lectures to displays and tours. As an example, one time when the Antelope Valley Ninety-Nines hosted the Southwest Section meeting, everyone was given an up-close inspection tour of the SR-71 Blackbird aircraft, located at Edwards Air Force Base. That experience, to me, was fascinating.

In 1996 the International Ninety-Nines hosted the World Precision Flying Competition at Meacham International Airport in Fort Worth, Texas, which was only the second time this event was held in the United States. The competition took place from September 30 through October 3, and support for this event was sought from the Ninety-Nines chapters from all over the country. Two members of the San Gabriel Valley chapter participated – Virginia Harmer and Penny. Virginia's husband, Dennis, and I went along to take part as fellow Forty-Nine and a Half volunteers. Our friend and nonpilot Kim Surh rode with us to offer whatever help she could.

We departed on Friday, September 27, as a flight of two, with Virginia and Dennis in their Cherokee and Penny, Kim, and me in our Mooney. Our destination for the first day was El Paso with a stop in Tucson for fuel and a pilot change. We spent the night in El Paso and continued on to Fort Worth in the morning, with a fuel stop and pilot change in Big Springs, Texas.

We arrived at Meacham Airport around midafternoon on Saturday after a smooth flight with clear skies. We had obtained advance hotel and rental car reservations before leaving on the trip. After arranging parking for our airplanes for the week, we unloaded our duffel bags and went into the terminal to look for the rental car counter. We were surprised to learn that there was none to be found. In fact, there were no rental car counters of any kind in the terminal. We called the company we had reserved with from the terminal and learned that, through a stroke of luck, their office happened to be in the hotel where we were staying, which was in downtown Fort Worth, and all of their rental-car check-ins were done there. We explained our situation, and the woman who was at the desk said she would come right out to pick us up.

When she arrived, we told her of the upcoming week's flying competition and said that the following day the airport would be inundated with people wanting rental cars. We had merely arrived a day early. This information came as news to her, as she hadn't heard of the pending international competition. But she was very customer focused. She apparently had some authority with that particular rental-car office, as she said that she would arrange for an all-day shuttle to take people from the airport to the hotel's rental car office. We reinforced her decision by emphasizing that several of the participants and volunteers would be arriving at different times and would be needing rental cars. Furthermore, the majority would be staying either at the same hotel as the rental car office or at hotels in the immediate area. Her company would receive considerable positive publicity by providing this service. Penny then suggested to her that it would be an excellent business move to install a counter in the Meacham terminal. Meacham was a fairly busy airport, and such an addition would likely pay off.

I must add as an aside that a couple of years later, we passed through the Meacham airport on our way home from a trip to Vermont. As we walked through the terminal, one of the first sights that caught our eyes was a rental-car counter for that very company, and there were several people at it. I nudged Penny and told her that she was responsible for that!

After our discussion with the rental-car lady, she took us to our hotel, where we checked out a rental car for the five of us and checked into our rooms. We spent the remainder of that day and most of Sunday exploring Fort Worth in preparation for the events beginning Monday.

The next four days were very busy for all of us. As a kickoff for the week's events, the twenty-two teams from around the world were treated on the first day to a parade and banquet at the Stockyards region of Fort Worth. The remaining three days of competitions were focused on navigations and landings. Everyone was at the airport by six in the morning for briefings and assignments, and we all were at our stations to begin judging by nine. All of us were split up and assigned to places where we were needed most. On the first day and a half of the actual competition, Penny and I were assigned to one of the navigation checkpoints where the participating pilots were to find our location and pass directly overhead using only dead reckoning techniques. Electronic navigational aids were not allowed. Our team had to drive for well over an hour to get to our station in time to set up. The pilot was supposed to fly directly over the large ground-target triangle we had spread out. To verify this, our team leader set up a makeshift sighting fixture whereby we could accurately track the overhead flights. This was great fun.

For the remainder of the competition, Dennis and I were assigned to judge landings. For the landing competition, a special pattern was taped off on the runway landing zone depicting where the wheels were supposed to touch down and stay down, without bouncing. We judges were to determine how close to the required touchdown point each pilot landed and grade accordingly. The execution of this function, however, required that we all stand directly at the edge of the runway. Dennis and I were on opposite sides of the runway, where we would hold up a banner to the approaching aircraft to identify the beginning of the landing zone. We would drop the banner just as the aircraft reached the marker. Hence, safety was a primary concern, as not all the competing pilots were of equal skill.

The person who served as the competition's safety judge and prevented any situation from arising that might lead to an accident was one of the more famous of the Ninety-Nines, Wally Funk. Many people may not be aware that at the time when the original seven astronauts were selected for the Mercury space program, there was a parallel effort initiated for women. Dr. William Lovelace, a former flight surgeon who helped develop the testing that would be required for NASA's male astronauts, was curious as to how women might perform on these same tests. After conducting a very successful preliminary test with a female pilot, Jerrie Cobb, he obtained private funding and, with the recruiting help of Cobb, reviewed the records of over seven hundred women pilots and invited several potential candidates to undergo these same tests. Thirteen women – all of whom were accomplished pilots with over one thousand hours of flight time – successfully underwent the same rigorous astronaut testing as that administered to the original seven men. All of these women, many of whom (and possibly all) were Ninety-Nines, qualified very favorably when compared with their male counterparts and came to be known as the Mercury 13.[16] Wally Funk was the youngest of the original Mercury 13 members, and both Penny and Virginia met her. Although all were well qualified, none of the Mercury 13 was selected for the astronaut program. The year 1960 was still in an era when cultural attitudes dictated that a woman's place was in an apron, not in space. Fortunately, times have changed.

The competition finished on Thursday, October 6, and a banquet was held that evening to celebrate the event and award medals to the winners. The following day we started our trek back home. Our plan for the return trip was to spend a couple of days in Albuquerque along the way. We would stop for lunch in Plainview, Texas, before continuing onward over the Sandia Mountains to Albuquerque International. The skies were partly cloudy as we left Meacham. But as we approached Plainview, the cloud cover was getting denser. There was a weather front coming our way. We landed at Plainville, fueled up, got a courtesy car from Miller Aviation, and went to lunch.

When we returned from lunch and turned in the courtesy car, we checked the weather for our flight to Albuquerque and found that the front was fast moving and had become solid IFR for the entire route. There was a convective Sigmet, a weather advisory for aircraft, sixty miles east of Albuquerque, telling us that we should also expect turbulence. Virginia had only recently acquired her IFR rating, and Penny and I both sensed that she seemed a bit unsure of making this flight. Penny put her at ease by suggesting that she go with Virginia in her plane and Dennis go with me in ours. Both Penny and I had flown this particular route in the

---

[16] Wikipedia. "Mercury 13," last modified July 22, 2019. https://en.wikipedia.org/wiki/Mercury_13.

past and were familiar not only with the airways but also with the landing patterns at Albuquerque. Virginia was greatly relieved, as this would be her first truly unfamiliar IFR route over mountains, and she would have an experienced copilot on board with her. Dennis was not instrument rated.

We called Flight Service and filed our IFR flight plans. I filed for the higher altitude of twelve thousand feet as our Mooney was turbocharged. Virginia and Penny took off first, and Dennis and I, with Kim in the backseat, followed. Although I had filed for twelve thousand feet, shortly after we had leveled off, the controller moved us up to fourteen thousand feet. The headwinds were considerably stronger at this altitude, plus we picked up occasional icing. Dennis had never experienced anything like this in the VFR world, so he was quite fascinated by this new environment.

When both planes got to the western side of the Sandia Mountains and we began our descents, we started to see breaks in the overcast. By the time we reached pattern altitude, we were able to make a visual approach into Albuquerque. We both taxied to the Cutter Aviation FBO for parking and fuel, and we arranged for a motel and rental car through them. The following day all four of us explored Old Town Albuquerque.

On Sunday we made our final leg home, with a fuel stop in Prescott. All the clouds had cleared out, leaving nothing but clear blue skies. It was a bit turbulent on the route back, however.

Penny's association with the Ninety-Nines had presented us with many aviation-related opportunities that we wouldn't have experienced otherwise. One in particular that would likely rate as our most unique experience of all our involvements was the chance to participate in a one-day training exercise in the altitude chamber at Edwards Air Force Base. One of the San Gabriel Valley Ninety-Nines had contacted officials at Edwards Air Force

Base and asked if it were possible for their chapter members to undertake this experience. To everyone's amazement and delight, permission was granted. A date for this activity was set up, and virtually everyone from the chapter participated.

The altitude chamber, or hypobaric chamber as it's often called, is essentially a large vacuum chamber with an internal pressure that can be accurately controlled to simulate specific altitudes. Air is pumped out of the chamber to simulate climbs to altitude and is allowed back in to simulate descents. Air crews undergo tests in a hypobaric chamber to gain experience with the effects of high altitude on the body, primarily to learn what their personal, specific hypoxia symptoms would be. The body experiences hypoxia when it is oxygen deficient, and it manifests in different ways for each person. By knowing what one's individual hypoxia symptoms are, in-flight oxygen emergencies can be averted.

Our altitude chamber experience started with a morning class, during which the entire procedure we would undergo was described. The instructor explained the proper use of the oxygen masks we all would be wearing, the altitude profiles the chamber would be taken to, how to perform the Valsalva process to equalize the pressure in our ears, and the physiological effects of hypoxia.

The Valsalva process involves closing one's mouth and pinching the nose while forcing air into the eustachian tubes of the ears. It's performed primarily during aircraft descents, when the outside air pressure builds up faster than is compensated by the inner ear. When in the chamber, we were instructed to yawn and pop our ears as the chamber pressure was being reduced, simulating a climb to the assigned altitude.

The instructor then discussed hypoxia, its symptoms, and how to recognize them. To name a few, symptoms can be confusion, change of skin color under nails to blue, cheeks becoming bright red, cough, rapid heart rate, shortness of breath, tingly lips, sweating, becoming giddy, and wheezing. The importance was that we identify what symptom is specific to us individually. After that, we played with the oxygen masks until we were comfortable that we had a good fit. Then we were ready for the chamber.

We all left the classroom for the adjoining room, where we were introduced to the altitude chamber. It was a fairly large facility that I would guess would comfortably seat sixteen people with eight on each side, and the ceiling was sufficiently high that we could stand upright. We all took a seat against either side of the chamber. Oxygen attachments were available at each station. The instructor showed us how to attach our oxygen masks and explained again what we were going to do. We donned our masks and breathed pure oxygen for a while before the chamber was closed to help purge nitrogen from our bodies so we wouldn't get the bends during our ascent. Then the chamber door was closed. Showtime!

The instructor told us that we would be doing two altitude profiles, the first one at ten thousand feet and the second at twenty-five thousand feet. We would ascend to the first profile, dwell there for a while, and then descend back to sea level. The primary purpose for this first step was to acquaint us with the effects of a fairly rapid altitude change and to allow us to properly equilibrate the pressure on our ears. Because we were all civilians being exposed to this for the first time, the instructor was sensitive to how everyone would react. In fact, one person did have a minor problem equilibrating ear pressure during the ascent, and the instructor stopped the climb until that person could successfully clear her ears. At ten thousand feet we took off our masks to see if we would feel any different. I didn't notice anything at that altitude, but I do seem to remember that the instructor had tied a rubber glove to the chamber ceiling prior to closing the door, and the rubber glove was inflated. We then put our masks back on and did the descent to practice our Valsalva.

The next ascent was to twenty-five thousand feet, and it was at this altitude where we would learn of the various physiological effects that altitude would have on us personally. As we went up in altitude, the instructor dimmed the lights in the chamber. Once we reached twenty-five thousand feet, we again took our masks off and were given a clipboard with a color wheel and a sheet of paper with a half dozen or so simple problems to solve. I don't remember the exact order in which we did these tests, but let's assume we started with the color wheel. With our masks off and breathing normally at this altitude with the lights dimmed, we were asked to look at the color wheel and identify the colors. That seemed very straightforward. I could see the reds, greens, and yellows and what looked like several gray segments. Then, with no other changes in the environment, the instructor had us put our masks back on. For me the entire color wheel lit up. It actually became brighter, although the light level in the room never changed. All the colors became clear – there were no grays. That was an awakening for me regarding the effect of oxygen deficiency on vision.

We took off our masks again and were instructed to answer the questions on the sheet. They were simple questions, like add two numbers, draw a hexagon, and so on. But as we were working down the list, the residual oxygen in our bodies was being depleted. The instructor reminded us when we took our masks off to be alert for symptoms of hypoxia while we were filling out this form. As for my own experience, as I was going down the list of questions on the form, I thought I was doing fine. However, my brain was getting a little foggy by the time I got to the very last question. I remember that question to this day. It was, "If the vice president dies, who is president?" I immediately started thinking of the government's chain of command and who came next after the vice president. Ah, the speaker of the house! I started to write that down, but something seemed out of place. Then it suddenly dawned on me that if the vice president dies, the president is still alive. The president is president. About then, I noticed that my lips were tingling. A dull brain and tingly lips are my hypoxia signs!

The instructor had us put our masks back on and turned up the lights. As we started descending to sea level, he again lectured us on Valsalva. Doing it correctly would be much more important this time due to our substantially greater pressure rise.

Once back at sea level, the door was opened. We all stood up, left our masks in our seats, and exited. We milled around and compared notes on our collective reactions. We all wanted to know what hypoxia symptoms we each felt and what we thought of the entire experience as a whole. One of the Ninety-Nines said that she started giggling when hypoxia was setting in, and I did remember hearing someone giggling after she mentioned that.

But all in all, this experience in the hypobaric chamber was unquestionably for me the most unique event in all of my aviation activities, and it would have never happened were it not for Penny's involvement with the Ninety-Nines. Most of the world likely believes that aviation is fundamentally a masculine endeavor. Perhaps it is. After all, as we indicated earlier, nearly 93 percent of all licensed pilots are male. But the women who do fly are a special breed. Just like the poem says, they know who they are, where they are, where they're going, and why. I found it both energizing and inspirational to be associated with and accepted by such a stimulating group – even though the highest rank I could ever achieve was Forty-Nine and a Half.

CHAPTER 4

EUPHORIA

What is it like to fly through the clouds
    And soar 'round a swirling tuft?

What do you feel as you drift in a dream
    Past a mountain of velvety fluff?

Can you explain the feeling you get
    As you glide through the canyons of wisp?

What is it like from the top of the world
    With your wingtips stirring the mist?

Tell me of the columns of billowy whiff
    That you glide so gracefully near.

Or of the puffy piles of delicate mounds
    That linger, then disappear.

What goes through your mind as you slip through the sky
    Past a bundle of dewy fleece?

Words can't be found, as none can describe
    The euphoria, your soul at peace.

Flying can be like a daydream when everything is smooth, and most of the time it is. A majority of our flights in one form or another mostly fell into this category. One of our most memorable examples occurred during a westbound flight over the western portion of the Arizona desert on a return flight from Phoenix. We were a few miles west of the White Tank Mountains when we approached a very large expanse of castellanus clouds, a field of tall columns of clouds with truncated bases terminating below our altitude and tops extending well above us. These cloud columns were about the width of our airplane and were spaced several airplane widths apart. Although such cloud formations typically are indicative of midatmospheric instability, the air was surprisingly smooth between them. Because we were on a VFR flight plan with flight following and had no immediate risk of flight conditions changing in front of us, we decided to weave around these columns of clouds as if we were flying around trees. The illusion created by the passing columns was like being on a magic carpet. The air traffic controllers who were watching our ground track were probably wondering what we were doing, however.

Every so often when we glide through the air, we find ourselves in nearly ideal flight conditions. The skies are clear, the air is fairly stable, and we have a tailwind. We experienced such an ideal occasion once during a flight to Denver. We had departed the Four Corners Regional Airport in Farmington, New Mexico, where we had spent the night, and were heading east for our climb over the Rockies. The airfield elevation at Four Corners is 5,506 feet, and the Rockies rise up very quickly east of there. Because the visibility was incredibly clear, we filed a VFR flight plan for 13,500 feet to go through the 11,000-foot pass west of Alamosa, New Mexico, and on to Pueblo, Colorado. We would then turn north to Denver from the east side of the mountains.

As we were climbing out of Farmington, we picked up a fairly strong tailwind, which aided our ascent immensely. If one were to visualize a large mass of air driving suddenly against the mountains, one can then readily understand how the air is pushed upward with considerable force, bringing everything with it — including airplanes. Even though our Mooney was turbocharged, the upwelling air gave us one of the fastest climbs we had ever experienced at that relatively high altitude. We reached our flight altitude considerably sooner than we had expected and began to level off. But the strong updrafts continued, so now our challenge was to maintain altitude and not be blown higher. Not a problem! We put the nose down to counter the updrafts and surfed across the Rockies. We maintained that attitude for what seemed like a good half hour, and the push from the mountain wave added a good thirty knots to our normal airspeed. The ride was fantastic!

Another incident of euphoria in flight, and very likely one of our most unforgettable, occurred one early October during our very first cross-country IFR flight to Vermont. Being our first-ever long trip, this flight presented us with many highlights. But the most significant occurred at the very end of the journey as we were given our descent instructions for our destination airport, the Edward F. Knapp State airport of Barre/Montpelier, Vermont.

We were with Boston Center for approach control details, and at our altitude we were generally on top of a very thick cloud layer. We received clearance from Boston Center to descend to four thousand feet and were given a vector for the direction in which we were to fly.

Everything was completely normal until we broke out of the clouds. As we did, our senses were shocked by a cacophony of color. Everywhere the eye could see over an area of several square miles was a blast of reds and oranges typical of Vermont during its first week of October. We were sufficiently taken by the sight before us that we momentarily forgot that we were on a controlled instrument flight course. But fortunately for us – this time – we were below the radar coverage of Boston Center, although we still had voice communications. The controller had no idea that we had strayed off course while being mesmerized by these incredible autumn colors. The controller's voice jolted us from our reverie when he asked if we had the airport in sight. I grew up in this part of the world and recognized the majority of the landmarks around where we were flying, so I had a fairly good idea of where the airport was relative to the direction we had drifted. I turned toward where I thought it would be and spotted it. I told the controller that we had the airport in sight and that landing was assured. I then canceled our IFR flight plan with him, and we descended among the color for a successful landing.

Many fliers might contend that aviation is like a religion. I would tend to agree. It has its many rituals and its gurus and high priests. And like all religions, it has its holy sites – its own Jerusalems, its Meccas. To general aviation, Mecca is Oshkosh, and participation in the annual fly-in to Oshkosh is the pilgrimage, or *hajj*. During one week of every year, typically around the end of July, the Wittman Regional Airport in Oshkosh, Wisconsin, becomes the busiest airport in the world. It has the highest concentration of airplanes in the air around it than any other airport. The event is the Experimental Aircraft Association (EAA) AirVenture Oshkosh. In 1993 we decided we were ready. That would be the year we would go on the *hajj*. Flying into Oshkosh for the AirVenture is a Rite of Passage.

But this particular trip would not be merely any flight or any typical fly-in to any given airport. This flight would require months of preparation. There are many rules and special steps that must be followed – and followed rigorously – for the arrival and landing at Oshkosh during that week. These rules and procedures are published months in advance in a special Notice to Airmen, or NOTAM.

NOTAMs normally are alerts issued by an aviation authority, such as the FAA, to notify pilots of potential hazards along a route of flight or at a specific location. That these potential hazards could affect the safety of the flight triggers the need for such an alert. Examples that would call for a NOTAM would be such instances as a runway closure at one's destination or parachute jumping along one's route. Large structures like tall towers in the vicinity of an airport would be another. Temporary NOTAMs that are expected to be in place for a very short time are sometimes referred to as temporary flight restrictions, or TFRs. For instance, whenever Air Force One visits Southern California, where we live, a TFR will invariably be issued that often affects the airspace near where our airplane was based, usually limiting access in certain quadrants. TFRs are normally lifted after a day or two. NOTAMs are a way of life in aviation, and when issued, they typically are only a page or two long.

The NOTAM for the EAA AirVenture, however, is upward of thirty-two pages! It informs the pilots of the reporting points they will acknowledge, the approaches into the airport they will use, the speed at which they will fly, the altitudes they will maintain, the airport departures they will use, the holds they will execute when the airport is closed, and virtually everything in between. This NOTAM is so intimidating that many pilots with more experience than we had will opt to land at an outlying airport and bus to Oshkosh.

We planned this trip with our friends Gordon and Shirley Hughes, and we would undertake it as a flight of two Mooneys. We contacted the AirVenture coordinators and requested the instruction package for an Oshkosh fly-in. I should point out that all of our plans were made in the days before the internet, so there was no website that we could access to download our required information. All correspondence was done by mail, and we were dependent upon the speed of the US Postal Service for our information material. So it took a week or so before we even had an idea of what would be required of us. But when the information package arrived, we got to work.

Although the specifics may have changed since then, one of the initial instructions for us was that we had to select our anticipated arrival time from a choice of time slots that were offered. I seem to remember that our window for arrival was fairly tight, like plus or minus an hour or so from our selected time. After the four of us consulted, we decided that we would plan to arrive on Sunday, August 1, which was also the opening day of the event that year. I don't remember the exact time we chose, but I believe it was around noon. Given this arrival estimate, we had to back up all of our flight legs and start times in order to make this fairly tight window. Considering that we had to fly nearly two thirds of the way across the country and still hit this very small time slot, the logistics for this trek had to be planned quite rigorously. To make this work and to ensure that we could meet our assigned window, we decided to select a layover airport within a couple of hours of Oshkosh, where we would land and wait until the remaining flight time from that airport would put us in Oshkosh on schedule. We picked Sioux City, Iowa.

The day finally arrived to begin our *hajj* to the holy city of Oshkosh. Because each Mooney was coming from a different location – Gordon and Shirley from San Jose and we from El Monte – we decided to meet in Rock Springs, Wyoming, and from there continue on to Scotts Bluff, Nebraska, where we would spend the night. So on Saturday, the last day of July 1993, Penny and I were wheels up for Cedar City, Utah, where we would make a fuel stop and change pilots. Once again we lucked out with the weather, as we had great VFR flight conditions for the entire distance.

Climbing out of Cedar City, we had a great view of the Wasatch Mountains as we flew past Park City, Utah, wending our way to Rock Springs, Wyoming. As part of our trip planning, we had coordinated an arrival time for Rock Springs. One of the uncanny traits, or personality flaws, of pilots is being on schedule. Both airplanes arrived at the Rock Springs Airport within minutes of each other. After fueling our planes, we had planned to have lunch right there at the airport, as earlier we had seen an advertisement for a restaurant on the field. But when we walked over to the restaurant, we found it was closed for remodeling, and the single vending machine had a very limited selection. Possibly because it was Saturday, there was no one around, so we decided to press on to Scotts Bluff, Nebraska, and have lunch there since we would be spending the night anyway. Tomorrow would be the big day. Tomorrow we were on to Oshkosh!

We got an early start the next morning in anticipation of an exciting day for all of us. The weather gods were kind to us again, as we were promised VFR weather all the way to Oshkosh. Right after breakfast, we checked out of our motel and headed off to the airport. Our plan was that Penny would fly us to Sioux City, and

I would be in the left seat for Oshkosh. Our strategy was to arrive in Sioux City in plenty of time to hit our tight arrival window at Oshkosh, and Sioux City was only about an hour and a half from Scotts Bluff, which would make it easy for us to adjust our timing appropriately to set that up.

We arrived in Sioux City with time to spare. We estimated that our arrival time at Oshkosh would be about two and a half hours from Sioux City, so we refueled our planes and dilly-dallied a bit until our estimated departure time for that window arrived. Immediately after takeoff, I contacted air traffic control for flight following to Oshkosh. With flight following, we would be in the system and given traffic advisories throughout the route of flight. And most importantly, we would be given a handoff to the proper radio frequency prior to our arrival at our first checkpoint. We were now on our way!

For the first hour or so we cruised along rather sedately, watching the scenery flow by. In this part of the country the land is fairly flat and marked by checkered wheat fields, dotted occasionally by grain elevators that slipped by below us. Our friends' Mooney was faster than ours, so they were in front of us. We lost sight of them for the remainder of this flight. We started to see occasional low scattered clouds the farther east we went, and off in the distance there was evidence of larger buildups, which could indicate a later thunderstorm. But the weather outlook was still calling for VFR conditions all the way to Oshkosh, so we didn't worry. Then within forty miles or so from Oshkosh we were awakened from our reverie by air traffic control, who gave us our new radio frequency and a vector to Ripon, Wisconsin – our first waypoint for landing at Oshkosh. We changed frequencies and checked in. It was showtime!

Because of the extreme volume of aircraft anticipated for this event, the lineup procedure for landing starts at the town of Ripon and requires visual navigation for the remainder of the flight. Ripon is about fifteen miles southwest of the Oshkosh airport, and the procedure calls for navigating from there by following a railroad track to a second waypoint at Fisk, Wisconsin. Landing runways and approach patterns are assigned by air traffic control at Fisk. We took a deep breath and started our approach to Ripon.

The arrival procedure also calls for very specific aircraft setup requirements prior to reaching Ripon. No closer than fifteen miles outside of Ripon, pilots are to ensure that their aircraft landing lights are turned on. The landing lights make each aircraft more obvious to all other air traffic. Then pilots must obtain the Oshkosh arrival ATIS, the Automated Terminal Information Service, on a separate frequency in order to learn the current airport conditions and which arrival runways are in use. After that, pilots are requested to monitor the Fisk Approach radio frequency. While all of this was taking place, we were required to descend to eighteen hundred feet altitude and reduce speed to ninety knots. And these were serious constraints. Ninety knots did not mean eighty-six knots or ninety-four knots; it meant ninety knots. We had to put our gear down to add additional drag in order to hold to the correct airspeed. Also, we were required to maintain at least a half mile spacing between aircraft. We made a guess at the distance, but I strongly suspect that most of us were a lot closer than a half mile.

By the time we arrived at Ripon, we had accomplished all of these steps and had locked in our altitude and speed. We entered the arrival procedure over the northeast corner of Ripon, following the railroad tracks. To ensure that we were on course, we were to look for grain elevators and a tall water tower to our left, which we saw. We had hit our target arrival window! So far so good!

While we were comfortably following the railroad tracks to Fisk and maintaining our speed and altitude, we were informed by Fisk Approach that the airport would be temporarily closed for a short air event and that everyone inbound to Fisk must now go into a hold pattern over Rush Lake. We had known that such an occurrence would be a possibility from the NOTAM, so we were prepared for it. The hold was to be left turns only and executed at the same altitude and airspeed we had been sustaining. So into the hold we went. It was at this point that I first became aware of the many other airplanes that were in our general vicinity. Having their landing lights on made them easier to spot. I don't really remember how long we were in the hold, but we did go around it several times.

When the all-clear notice was given, we completed and departed the hold and proceeded on to Fisk. As we approached Fisk, we were issued our runway assignment, our transition route, and the tower frequency to monitor. On the tower frequency we were told by the air traffic controllers to listen up and shut up. The frequency would be too busy for them to handle responses, unless we didn't understand their instructions. Several controllers with binoculars were stationed on the ground along the route. They would identify us by aircraft type and color, or N number if they could see it, and we would respond by rocking our wings. We were instructed to continue following the railroad track until reaching the point where it intersects the highway, which would mark the downwind entry to Runway 27, our assigned landing runway. The density of the air traffic around us was now becoming obvious. I had never seen so many airplanes in the air in one place before. Even though everyone was at the correct speed and altitude, it was still an impressive sight. Air traffic controllers were barking instructions at a terrific rate. I heard afterward that controllers volunteer for this event at Oshkosh just for the experience of working extremely heavy traffic, and only the best are selected.

We entered downwind for Runway 27 in the trail of what looked like a Cessna 152, a two-seat airplane. I looked around for a moment at all the airplanes in front of us that were turning to base leg and then to final. The controllers were sounding more and more like auctioneers, instructing planes when to turn to base leg or to extend downwind slightly before turning and so on. When our turn came to turn to base, everything went smoothly. As the Cessna in front of us turned final, it was instructed to land short – in other words, to land on the numbers. As we turned final behind it, we were instructed to land long – to not touch down until we were halfway down the runway. That would give the Cessna time to get off the runway as we passed overhead of it. The Oshkosh airport is laid out with a complex set of runways. Perpendicular to Runway 27, our assigned runway, and displaced from it by nearly a half mile is Runway 18, a longer runway for larger aircraft. I mention this because as we were passing over the Cessna that had already touched down, a large twin-engine airplane passed over us. For a moment we were in a three-plane stack! Then we too touched down. We had arrived at Mecca.

We left the active runway at one of the many designated exits and followed the cones and the countless volunteers aligning the makeshift taxiways that would take us out into the adjoining fields for parking. The volunteers had the parking procedure so well in hand that it was like parking a car at a major concert or sports event. It seemed like we taxied forever across this vast field. Airplanes were parked everywhere, and many of them, especially the high wings, were set up as temporary campsites with tarps draped over their wings. And there was evidence that it had rained recently. This was the first time we noticed it. The large mass of cloud buildup in the east we had seen as we flew in was the likely cause, and lucky for us it had moved on.

The army of volunteers guided us down a grassy lane and finally directed us into a parking slot. In order to accommodate the maximum number of airplanes, all planes were being parked two deep, facing each other. It was only then as we turned right and aligned our wings with the adjoining airplane that we noticed that we were directly across from Gordon and Shirley's Mooney. They had arrived before us and were already out of their plane, watching us park. We were parked nose to nose – spinner to spinner with them. What a coincidence! There is no way we could have ever planned this.

We unloaded our airplane, tied it down, and covered it, as this was to be its home for the next few days. By now it was late afternoon and warm. The massive buildup of billowing clouds in the east added a dramatic punctuation to a very exciting day. Everything that had to do with this event was very well organized, and this included a constant flow of shuttles for ground transport. We all picked up our gear and walked over to one of the shuttle stops to board a shuttle that would take us to the event's main entrance. It was only then that I glanced upward and saw the long line of arriving aircraft on the downwind approach to landing. Airplanes upon airplanes just kept coming. It was surreal!

As part of our overall planning for this trip, we had arranged to stay in one of the dormitories of the University of Wisconsin–Oshkosh campus, which was fairly close by. And there were buses running on a regular schedule all day between the university and the main entrance for the AirVenture.

Our shuttle from our parking space dropped us off very close to the regular bus stop where we could catch the bus to the university and other points within the city itself. All ground transportation was free during this week. After a short wait, we got on the bus that took us directly to the university. Once there, we located the office area that coordinated the dorm assignments and found our home for the week. We checked in, dropped off our things, met up, and found a place to eat. Tomorrow would begin a week of total immersion in aviation.

Staying at the university dorm in Oshkosh was a reminder of my undergraduate days. The room was equipped with two single beds and two desks, and the bathrooms and showers were down the hall, conveniently separated for men and women. There was one openable window. Adjacent to the dorm within very easy walking distance were several standard-fare fast-food restaurants. Very little had changed since my undergraduate days, except that the dorms I had lived in were for men only.

The next morning after breakfast we were back on the bus heading for the main entrance of the AirVenture. Once there, we each bought a full week's pass that allowed us into all the events. We didn't want to miss anything. And in we went.

The AirVenture Oshkosh, without exaggeration, has to be the world's largest aviation event. Attendance is well over a half million people, including over ten thousand aircraft that actually fly into the airport itself. And this attendance includes more than two thousand people registered from eighty or more countries. The year we were there, we learned later, an acquaintance of ours from Switzerland had flown his Mooney across the Atlantic to attend. This one week per year at Oshkosh is the world's greatest celebration of wings, and anything and everything with wings can be found there. Everything from the futuristic ultramoderns to the ultralights, from warbirds to home-builts, from the giant C-5 to the paraglider – every conceivable, imaginable thing that could somehow get off the ground can be found at Oshkosh. They're all there on display. Simultaneously, aviation lectures are given nearly continuously in various tents, workshops and demonstrations are put on for those who want to build their own airplanes, and air shows occur virtually nonstop. For five days straight we were totally submerged in aviation.

But all good things must end, and five days later the show was over; it was time to leave. Departing Oshkosh is almost as complex as arriving. First, there was to be no aircraft engine started until the pilots had listened to the Departure ATIS, and then they were to taxi to the designated runways following a series of nearby flagmen's instructions without contacting ground control. Air traffic controllers, who were wearing pink shirts for ease of identification, were positioned on elevated platforms near the runway departure points. And airplanes were taking off from both sides of the runway centerline, virtually two at a time. The four of us took our time getting to the airport on departure day. But when we did arrive, we watched with our jaws dropped as this spectacle unfolded. Everything was well executed and completed without incident.

By the time we ourselves were ready to leave, the field in which thousands of planes had been parked for the past few days was almost empty. Way off in the distance were two Mooneys sitting by themselves, nose to nose. The show was now over, and ours were the last two parked planes. We gathered up all of our belongings and started walking toward them. When we got to the airplanes, we called out for a fuel truck to top us off before we departed.

Once in the air and heading west, and again on flight following, we had been alerted from our earlier weather briefing to be on the lookout for deteriorating weather conditions along our route. As we approached the Mississippi River, we commented on the muddied fields below us indicative of the rather extensive flooding that had occurred a few weeks earlier when the river overflowed its banks. We also noted the worsening visibility in front of us, so we turned to fly south along the river to see if there would be any improvement. Since our two Mooneys were in radio contact with each other, we decided that if the visibility didn't improve then, we should air-file IFR for landing at Waterloo, Iowa, for fuel. The weather did not improve, so we turned west and contacted air traffic control at Chicago Center and got our IFR flight plan.

Once we attained the altitude and heading assigned by Chicago Center and had settled in for the cruise, we looked through our on-board paperwork for the Waterloo IFR approach plates and airport diagram. An approach plate is a chart of the step-down instructions that a pilot follows to enable safe arrival at an airport by referring solely to the aircraft instruments when in weather conditions for which the pilot has no outside visual reference. We came up empty. We did not have the Waterloo approach plates on board. In fact, we had no airport information of any kind for the entire state of Iowa.

I called over to Gordon on our preselected frequency and told him of our dilemma. I mentioned to him that as soon as we were transferred to the Waterloo Approach frequency, I would be first to contact Waterloo Approach and would ask the controller to read off the landing procedure for me to copy. We had our fingers crossed that the controller would be willing to do that, or we would have to ask for vectors for descent and landing. And we were not sure how that would work.

When we were transferred to Waterloo Approach, I did just that. I told the controller that we didn't have the approach plates and asked him if he would be willing to tell me what the approach instructions were. He chuckled and said it was not a problem. There was virtually no other radio traffic, and he was not all that busy. He gave us an option of what approach we would like, and we chose a VOR approach as being likely the simplest to copy. The

Waterloo airport has three separate runways on which we could land from either end, and the VOR is on the field in the middle of all three. I don't remember specifically which one he assigned us. But since we were generally westbound and he had us fly to the VOR first, I suspect that he assigned us Runway 12 as being the easiest for us to enter and set up. His instructions for us were the following:

> Navigate to the Waterloo VOR, on frequency 112.2, follow it outbound on a 313-degree heading while descending to 2,800 feet. Execute a procedure turn to a 268-degree heading and return on a 088 degree heading to intersect the VOR 313-degree radial and track inbound, heading 133 degrees. Descend inbound to 1,500 feet and advise when airport is in sight. If airport is not in sight, then execute a missed approach, which is a climbing left turn to 3,300 feet to intersect the VOR radial 096 outbound to the DEWAR[17] intersection and hold. DEWAR is on the Cedar Rapids 332-degree radial on frequency 114.1.

Both Penny and I scrambled to take all of this down, and I asked him to read it back to us at least once, maybe twice. When we thought we had all the steps, I read it to him. He said that was it and to proceed on for landing.

---

[17] The enroute intersections of major airways are typically defined by five-letter designations that are pronounceable. Often an IFR pilot is called upon to identify when reaching such an intersection before executing the next instruction, as would be the case for DEWAR.

As soon as I got off the radio, Gordon came on the frequency and requested an IFR approach to landing. Then he added, "And I've got the approach plate!"

The controller came back on and said, "That's great! Can you fax a copy of it over to the Mooney in front of you?"

We all laughed out loud at that one.

The air around the airport was calm and the cloud bases were fairly high, so we had no problem sighting the runway once we broke out of the overcast. We landed uneventfully and taxied for fuel. Once on the ground, all four of us had a second laugh when relating this experience.

At this point we took a break for lunch and to check the weather outlook for conditions west of us. There was a line of storms moving southwest from Colorado along our route of flight, and we decided that it would be wise if we made North Platte, Nebraska, our destination for that day and spent the night there. By morning the storm front was expected to have moved east from Nebraska and would be behind us. So we filed an IFR flight plan and departed Waterloo westbound for North Platte. The flight took us a little over three hours, during which we were "in the soup" with actual instrument conditions for a good hour and a half.

After breakfast the following morning, we all headed back to the airport, where the two Mooneys would be departing ways. Gordon and Shirley would be going to San Jose from there, while we were planning to stop at Centennial Airport in Denver to visit friends for the weekend prior to continuing on home.

It was a great VFR flight from North Platte to Denver, wending our way around the many residual clouds left over from the storm that passed through the day before. Once at Centennial, however, the tower controller got a bit confused when we and one other Mooney called in about the same time for landing. So we helped him out by opting for Runway 28, the side runway. Since we had been there before, we were familiar with this airport, whereas the other Mooney pilot apparently was not.

We spent the next two evenings with our friends before continuing our final trek home. On the morning of August 8, we were back at Centennial, preparing for our departure with plans for a fuel stop and pilot change at Farmington, New Mexico, our favorite stop on the west side of the Rockies. From Farmington we made a second stop in Needles, California, after dodging cloud buildups, flying through a few rain squalls, and experiencing a bit of turbulence typical of the summer desert thermals. The skies were clear all the way from Needles to El Monte. Our wheels touching down on Runway 19 at El Monte was like an exclamation point, punctuating the grand finale of one of our greatest flying adventures ever!

The feeling one gets from flight is the very definition of euphoria. Fundamentally, that's what flying for pleasure is all about. It allows one to momentarily defy gravity and ascend to a higher level of being, both physically and spiritually. While physically above the ground and drifting with no obvious support, the pilot is spiritually in a new dimension, unconstrained by the mundane, untethered by the now. He has become a Sky Walker.

CHAPTER 5

IFR to Bradford

We were an hour out of Bradford
In a sky black as a well.
We'd just been given a vector north
To avoid a fast-moving cell.

The lightning from off our right
Told us how close we were.
Its flash interrupted the noise of the rain
And the steady engine purr.

The drone was broken by a controller's voice
As the radio crackled on.
"We're painting another in front of you,
But you'll pass it before too long."

"How's the weather farther ahead?
Will we be breaking clear?"
"It's looking good in twenty miles.
Scattered clouds should soon appear."

The lightning flash in front of us
Told us to cinch down tight.
But we had a pretty good tailwind,
So with luck it would stay on our right.

We droned on for a little while
As the plane got tossed about,
But it wasn't too much longer
When it started to settle out.

The weather guesser was right this time,
And a clearing appeared as he said.
But a new front coming up from the south
Was occluding with ours up ahead.

We broke out beside a towering cloud
That billowed like a fleecy mound,
And dialed in the Bradford ASOS
As we continued inward bound.

The ASOS reported Bradford was clear
With winds no greater than ten.
That this was not even close to correct
We had no idea right then.

Cleveland Center came back on the line
And descended us to four.
But the clouds and wind all around us said
To check ASOS once more.

A ceiling of five hundred was suddenly there,
As was a forty-knot squall!
"You're cleared for the VOR DME arc,"
Said the Cleveland Center drawl.

"Negative on the DME arc,
The winds are too severe.
We'll take the VOR alpha,
And shoot the approach from there."

"You're cleared for the VOR alpha.
Your decision is probably sound.
Get back to me, one two four point three
Or cancel on the ground."

The winds were from the south-southeast
And blowing up a gale.
We were lucky that the rain was warm
Lest the plane be pelted with hail.

We turned in toward the VOR,
Crabbing into the tempest's rage.
The bumpy ride made it really tough
Centering the needle in the gauge.

The wind was so strong at the VOR
That the turn to the outward bound
Took nearly 180 degrees
To get the plane completely around.

The trip out to the procedure turn
Was as fast as a thunder crack.
We were swept along like a featherweight
With the wind now at our back.

But around the turn it was not the same
With the wind now on our face.
Tracking inbound, we seemed to stop
And hover, suspended in space.

We passed the final approach fix
In that dark and turbulent cell,
But descending to the decision height
Broke out – five hundred AGL.

The runway was right in front of us
And visibility was clear for miles.
GUMPS was checked and all was well –
We couldn't resist the smiles.

The mains touched smoothly on the runway
Like the kiss of a summer breeze,
And the speed dropped off so gently
We made the turnoff with ease.

We taxied to transient parking,
And unloaded our stuff for the night.
We told the old-timers in the office nearby,
"Your ASOS isn't working right!"

The one with his elbow on the counter
Chuckled to us and said,
"That ASOS ain't been working for a time,
And the new one's still in the shed.

"But we listened to you on the radio
And we heard you pass overhead.
We watched out the window while you landed.
You did very well!" he said.

"A lady's voice on the speaker
Got us curious what you would do.
The King Air that landed earlier
Wasn't half as good as you.

"He bounced twice on the runway
Then skidded from left to right.
But you put your wheels straight on the ground
And held the plane down tight.

"Hat's off to you lady pilots
From all of us who care.
You who gracefully pilot an aircraft
Without need for the macho air!"

This is a true story. It occurred on September 29, 1999, with Penny in the left seat flying into Bradford, Pennsylvania. Our flight conditions for this story were under IFR conditions. In fact, the cloud density in this circumstance was so thick that for most of that leg of the flight, we couldn't even see our wingtips. Our only means of situational awareness was through the primary flight instruments mounted in the front panel of the aircraft – hence "instrument" flight rules. This poem also introduces phrases, or jargon, that are specific to those flight conditions, and I'll explain their meaning. In fact, in this chapter I will define unfamiliar terms in much more detail than I have done so in previous or subsequent chapters.

First, when flying IFR, pilots are always in radio contact with an FAA specialist on the ground who is in front of a radar screen conducting air traffic control, whether it be an approach control, where pilots are given flight directions pertinent to traffic in and around nearby larger-use airports, or whether it be in the jurisdiction of a flight-control center that controls a very large area. In this instance, we were communicating with Cleveland Center. The radio is a pilot's link to the outside world when flying in the soup, and on that day we were doing just that.

One of the nice services that air traffic control provides for IFR flights in rough weather is to let pilots know if there is a major thunderstorm cell on their flight paths. If they are painting such a cell on their radar, they will give pilots a vector around it. A vector is an assigned direction, and we had just received that assignment to turn north to go around such a cell as our story starts out.

We were eastbound at seven thousand feet with a fairly good tailwind, and there was a northeasterly progressing frontal system moving fairly rapidly, with cells converging on us from the south. We could see the flashes of lightning being generated by those cells off to the right side in front of us. The needle of one of our instruments, the automatic directional finder or ADF, would jump toward the direction of the flash, responding to radio frequencies generated by the lightning, so we had a fairly good idea where it was coming from.

Our goal was to land at the airport in Bradford, Pennsylvania, where we would spend the night. The flight controller told us that we would be flying out of the densest part of the clouds fairly shortly into conditions where we would be popping in and out of clouds for the remainder of the trip. However, the fast-moving frontal system to our south was a cold front, and it was joining a second warm-frontal system just southeast of Bradford. The result was an occluded front, which for us meant that we were probably going to encounter some significant turbulence. And we were not disappointed! The winds became very strong as we approached the occlusion.

At the point when we were within twenty miles of the Bradford airport, we started to prepare our landing procedures, and the very first step in these procedures is to find out what the local weather conditions are at the airport. These local reports give us the wind directions and the preferred runway to use. For a tower-controlled airport, pilots set a radio frequency for that airport's ATIS, which is a continuous broadcast of that airport's winds, visibility, and general landing conditions. But Bradford's airport was uncontrolled, meaning it had no tower. For landing advisories, most uncontrolled airports also have some form of automated system that gives a continuous output of local landing conditions, similar to the ATIS, and that's typically an Automated Surface Observing System, or ASOS. Furthermore, at uncontrolled airports pilots rely upon themselves and others to announce their positions to any other air traffic that might be in the area. They do this on a radio communication frequency that has been specifically assigned to that airport by the FAA. All of these frequencies are found on the aviation charts for each specific airport.

At the time of our flight to Bradford, many of these uncontrolled airports were converting over to the upgraded ASOS. And during this transition period, many of us pilots had observed that the ASOS systems were not all that reliable. Part of the reason for this unreliability was that the sensor was seeing only what was directly above it. For example, if there were a small clearing in the clouds, it would see the weather as clear. Fortunately, these instruments have been greatly improved since these early trial periods. However, when we heard the Bradford ASOS report that skies were clear and winds were calm, we were very suspicious and decided not to believe it.

While all of this was happening, Cleveland Center was starting to line us up for our landing approach into the airport.

In doing this, they assigned us altitudes to fly. And since we were at seven thousand feet, we were instructed to descend to four thousand feet – the reference in the poem is "descended us to four." Because we were suspicious of the last ASOS reading, we went back to it. This time we got something much more realistic! It was now reporting a low ceiling and strong winds, and we believed it. As we approached the region of the occluded fronts, we started to pick up some very strong winds and found it necessary to add an exceptionally large wind correction in order to maintain our course. *Wind correction* refers to the angle at which the pilot must put the nose of the aircraft relative to the desired flight direction in order to correctly remain on course. Not doing so would cause the aircraft to be blown off course, into a direction unauthorized for IFR. Our wind correction was so exaggerated that we were essentially flying sideways – left wing forward! This flight configuration is referred to as crabbing. The good news in all of this was that the winds at this point were not especially turbulent, just strong, and we could maintain our orientation fairly well.

Now that we had the plane properly oriented and were flying directly toward the navigational aid, which in this case was a very high frequency omnidirectional range system, or VOR, Cleveland Center came back on the radio and cleared us to execute a fairly complex approach to set us up for landing. We were cleared to do the VOR distance-measuring equipment (DME) arc approach that would line us up with the runway. In this approach, the pilot flies a semicircle to maintain a fixed distance from the VOR, as determined by the DME, installed in the airplane's instrument panel. This fixed distance is typically ten miles. Accurately holding this distance while in IFR conditions can be a little tricky at times, and with the winds we were experiencing, it would have been extremely difficult. So we declined this clearance and requested the more standard VOR approach, which we were given.

At this point we had to transfer our communications from Cleveland Center to the common traffic advisory frequency, or CTAF, for Bradford so as to announce our positions and determine whether other aircraft were in the area. Since we would be changing frequencies from Cleveland Center, the final instruction to us was in reference to canceling our IFR flight plan. If we had been landing at a towered airport, such cancellation would be automatic. But since the Bradford airport was uncontrolled (i.e., without a tower), the onus was upon us to actively cancel our plan. And for this, there were two options. Once we knew that our landing was assured, we could recontact Cleveland Center and tell the controller we were canceling IFR, or we could call Flight Service once on the ground and cancel through them. We had selected to do the latter. Hence, the last instruction from Cleveland Center was to give us the frequency on which to call center back for the flight plan cancellation or the option to cancel through Flight Service on the ground.

But now the fun began! As we approached the VOR to execute our turn, it started to rain and we ran into some moderate turbulence. We agreed that Penny would concentrate on flying the plane and that I would focus on the navigation. In the past we have found this to be an excellent combination, as I am usually very good with situational awareness. She was holding the plane steady through all of this, but it now took nearly her total concentration. Since we were severely crabbed as we got closer to the VOR and the nose was pointed in almost the opposite direction of where we needed to go, she had to bring the nose much farther around than one might normally expect. The total extent of this turn would be counterintuitive if we were not completely aware of our orientation. All this time we were still in the clouds.

With the turn completed, we were now flying outbound from the VOR over the runway even though we couldn't yet see it. But did we ever pick up a tailwind! All that crabbing we had done to hold our course now put the wind directly at our back. We timed our outbound leg, executed our procedure turn to line up with the runway, and began our final descent. A procedure turn is a special maneuver that allows the plane to leave its course, execute a turn, and reacquire the course in the opposite direction without pilots' losing their bearings.

Facing the runway, we now were experiencing a very strong headwind that abruptly slowed us down, giving us the illusion of standing still.

We passed the reference point indicating it was now safe to descend – the "final approach fix" – and began our descent. We broke out of the clouds around five hundred feet above ground level, 500 AGL, to a visibility that was crystal clear. The runway was right in front of us. Penny put the landing gear down, configured the flaps for landing, and checked the GUMPS, an acronym that virtually every pilot uses as a mental checklist to verify that the airplane is set up for a safe landing. The *G* is for *gas*: Is the fuel selector on the correct tank? The *U* is for *undercarriage*: Is the landing gear down? *M* is for *mixture*: Is the fuel mixture properly set for lower altitude? *P* is for *propeller*: Is the propeller configured for landing? And finally, *S* is for *switches* and *seat belts*: Are the switches in their proper positions, such as the electric fuel pump turned on? Is everyone's seat belt securely fastened?

All this time Penny was announcing her position from the outbound leg, through the procedure turn inbound, and on short final, when we were within a half mile of landing. She then made a perfect landing.

Once the plane slowed sufficiently on the runway, she took a taxiway off-ramp, announced her position and intentions, and

SPIRIT OF THE SKY WALKERS

taxied to transient parking, where we would be parked for the night. She taxied up to and alongside a twin-engine King Air and shut down the engine. We unloaded our overnight bag from the plane and walked into the office of the adjacent FBO, where we would phone Flight Service to cancel our IFR flight plan. The FBO was manned by two retired gentlemen.

As we were signing in, we told the FBO operators about their faulty ASOS, and they really did chuckle about it. They were aware of the problem, but so far they had not gotten around to replacing it with the upgraded unit that they had on hand. But at this point they offered a very nice compliment to Penny's radio work and airmanship in handling the landing. Anyone who has ever handled a Mooney knows that it's a complex airplane with aerodynamic characteristics that require it be flown all the way to the ground. And that applies to optimum conditions. However, the flight conditions we experienced were far from optimum, yet Penny handled it masterfully. This impressed both FBO operators, and they were very complimentary to her!

They should have witnessed the landing she had made a couple of years earlier in San Antonio. During that landing, the wind sock was straight out and perpendicular to the runway. Penny had both the airplane wing dipped low with full opposite rudder and the nose crabbed into the wind, and she put it down on one wheel, straightened the nose, and continued the rollout. We never felt a bump.

A flight such as the one of our poem is not for the faint of heart or even for the recently ordained instrument pilot. But by the time we had taken this particular trip, we had accumulated considerable similar experience such that no single incident we encountered was really new to us. However, one of the lessons this might offer to the newly minted instrument pilot is the importance of maintaining situational awareness when in the

97

soup. By watching the aircraft's instruments and imagining the plane's track across the ground, we were able to correctly ascertain the airplane's orientation to its desired course. Admittedly, the majority of today's airplanes will likely be equipped with global positioning satellite, or GPS, receivers with moving-map displays that clearly show the aircraft's orientation, position, and ground reference. All one needs to do is look at it. It couldn't be easier.

But what if there were an electrical failure and that feature were not available? One must always be prepared for that eventuality and do what we did. We had no GPS moving-map display. Our only moving-map reference was the one that played out in our minds. Only our imaginations displayed the aircraft's orientation, position, and ground reference. But anything different wouldn't be any fun for a Sky Walker.

CHAPTER 6

THE LEGEND OF BARNEY BELLOU

There's a legend known in County Malone
Of a flyer named Barney Bellou,
And that stormy night when he flew out of sight
In a Waco of robin's-egg blue.

Young Billy Karhn fell from the barn,
His Life Force ebbing away.
"By the hands of the clock, if he don't see a doc,
He won't make it through the day!

"The road to town is rough and wound
All rutted this time of year.
And the town of Skiles is like a hundred miles,
Way too far, I fear.

"That storm in the West rates with the best
And it's right smack dab in our way.
We better be quick! It's here in a lick
And it looks like it's fixin' to stay!

"Get on the phone to the aerodrome
And see who's around tonight!
There must be one brave son of a gun
Who's willin' to make a flight!"

The call came in amidst the din
Of an engine's shutdown knock.
"Hey, you out there! Could you take to the air
And take an injured kid to a doc?"

"I'm Barney Bellou, and my Waco'll get through.
I know every inch of that pass.
Have a medical team at the old Conner stream
And I'll set 'er right down on the grass."

They cinched Billy in with the belt past his chin
His poor body all broken askew.
His time left still depends on the skill
Of this stranger named Barney Bellou.

The Waco's core jumped with a roar
As the first bolt of lightning flew.
Dark clouds poured down as the wheels left the ground,
Swallowing the lone craft and its crew.

Trees passed so near to the landing gear
Their tips touched the belly of blue.
Not a single light on that darkest of night
Guided brave Barney Bellou.

The Hammer of Thor fell sharply before
The turbulent Waco's path.
The thunder's clash and lightning's flash
Spewed violence with a vengeful wrath.

Rain became hail and began to impale
Like stingers on the face of our crew.
Yet he stayed the course like an old plow horse
That mysterious Barney Bellou.

His course held stead with the coolest of head
Like one on a mission possessed.
His ghostly calm in this ghastly storm
Was more real than could ever be guessed.

One had to stare to see the faint flare
That marked the spot to come down.
But Barney just knew it and was gliding down to it –
The only clear spot on the ground.

The wind was chilly as they pulled out Billy.
"Who's the brave soul who brought you through?"
A weak voice said through a foggy head,
"His name is Barney Bellou."

The old doc turned pale as a pellet of hail.
Something was terribly wrong!
Then he turned to see where Barney would be –
But Barney Bellou was gone!

"Billy, your host was Barney's ghost!
His spirit is what brought you through.
He met his fate back in '38
When flying was kinda new.

"His very last flight was this same kind of night
With the Storm Gods stirring their brew.
Topped off with gas and heading for the pass
Was the last glimpse of Barney Bellou.

"We searched days on end, our hopes grew thin,
He was nowhere at all to be found.
For all we know, or can ever show,
He's still out there flying around.

"But to this day folks still say,
When the thunder clouds abound,
If you listen clear, you maybe can hear
A muffled engine sound.

"His spirit's been adrift in a timeless rift
Awaiting its call tonight.
With that awesome mass closing over that pass,
Only Barney could have made that flight.

"I don't know for sure, but I've said it before,
The mysteries of life are vast.
Your trip tonight may have been his last flight.
Barney's ghost may be resting at last."

The intent of "The Legend of Barney Bellou" was to conjure up the image of flight as it was in its early years, the era of the barnstormers, the time when entrepreneur pilots would fly from town to town, landing in fields and selling afternoon airplane rides to the townsfolk who would turn out. The Waco was selected for this story because it was a popular biplane of the 1930s, sporting two open cockpits; the pilot normally sat in the rear one with the passenger sitting in the front.

Flying in an airplane with an open cockpit brings with it all the adventure and glamour of those early days. With feet on the rudder pedals and gently pushing harder with the left while slightly nudging the stick held between the knees to the left to execute a shallow turn, one can peer over the side to look at the ground passing below. The wind can be felt on one's face as it's heard whistling through the wing struts. This environment provides the true feeling of flying like no other, a feeling of being suspended above the world and slipping among the clouds, truly free from the bonds of gravity.

Many people may not fully realize that the barnstormers arrived less than two decades after the airplane itself. The airplane was born at Kitty Hawk on a cold December morning in 1903 when the Wright brothers showed the world that powered flight was feasible. And like the birth of a gazelle on the Serengeti, the airplane was no sooner on its feet than it was running and bounding, finding its niche in its new life. The advent of World War I barely over a decade later dramatically accelerated its growth, specifically its airframe and engine developments. By the time the war was over, a mere fifteen years after the airplane's first-ever flight, the airplane had emerged into the stable, three-axis-controlled configuration that is recognized today. Many of the recently discharged army pilots bought surplus Curtiss JN-4 "Jenny" biplanes that the government was selling for as little as $200 apiece and started the barnstorming craze. Since the JN-4 Jenny was a trainer aircraft in which virtually every US aviator from World War I had learned to fly, it was familiar to the returning servicemen who wanted to own their own aircraft and continue with their newly found passion.

In the early era of the barnstormers, only a special person took to the air, a person who symbolized the epitome of bravery. So much was unknown about the skies in that era that even for experienced pilots, venturing far from one's home base was analogous to the experience of the ancient seafarers venturing out of sight of their home coastlines. Weather patterns could change quickly, and the winds aloft were different from the winds on the ground. There were hills and mountains to navigate around, with unfamiliar updrafts and downdrafts. Clouds could suddenly appear from nowhere and confuse our gallant aviators. To add even more uncertainty to this matter, the airplane equipment itself was not all that reliable. Engine development was new and subject to failures, and navigational aids were yet to be invented.

Yet even in the face of all these unknowns, during the early to mid-1920s, barnstormers fired the imaginations of thousands and provided one of the most awe-inspiring forms of enjoyment. Furthermore, since barnstorming itself became a loosely organized aviation function, it entered the annals of flight history as the first major category of civil aviation. To the recently discharged army pilots, who acquired their love of the air from their experiences in the war, barnstorming offered them a means to continue this exciting pursuit while simultaneously enabling them to earn a living. Equipped with a recently purchased government-surplus Jenny, the barnstormers would set off either by themselves or as members of a small team for a small rural town. They would find a local field that seemed suitable as a base of operations, land there, and then ask permission of the local owner to use the field as a make-shift runway for offering airplane rides or to put on an airshow – or both. Then they would return to the town and fly over it low and slow to attract the townsfolks' attention, either by dropping leaflets or by merely buzzing the town itself. One must keep in mind that in this era, the vast majority of people had never seen an airplane, say nothing of seeing it do the loop-the-loop, do barrel rolls, or see people walking out onto the wings while the plane flew by. These events were so popular that local businesses would close shop to allow everyone to attend the shows.[18]

During this era of aviation infancy when there were no regulations governing any aspect of aviation, barnstormers had complete freedom to do whatever they wanted. And that they did. In addition to charging a small fee for airplane rides, they also staged some of the most daring airshows, such as aerobatics very close to the ground, simulated aerial combat, and flying through open barn doors.

As barnstorming itself caught on, groups of pilots would often team up and form what came to be called flying circuses. They would tour the country performing such various daredevil feats as flying upside down, wing walking, and changing planes in midflight. Some of the most famous names in aviation started out in barnstorming as stunt pilots. Included among these people are Charles Lindbergh, Wiley Post, Pancho Barnes, and Roscoe Turner.

The advent of the Air Commerce Act in 1926, however, brought about the formal regulation of aviation, requiring pilots and planes to be licensed and flight safety constraints to be imposed. The new safety regulations demanded that flight equipment meet certain minimum safety standards and that aerial stunts be performed at higher altitudes. These restrictions not only imposed financial hardships on the casual barnstormer, but the requirement that aerial tricks be performed at much higher altitudes meant that they became less thrilling to the observers on the ground. This situation was further exacerbated by several highly publicized accidents resulting from increasingly dangerous

[18] Wikipedia. "Barnstorming," last modified July 12, 2019. https://en.wikipedia.org/wiki/Barnstorming.

stunts, acts that begged for more rigorous safety constraints. And the government's decision to stop selling Jennies in the late 1920s didn't help. These new rules made conventional barnstorming very difficult to sustain and essentially led to its demise.

The most challenging aspect of early flight was getting from Point A to Point B. While overall airframe and engine development advanced and reliability improved considerably during World War I, navigation was still very primitive. Navigational instruments consisted of barely more than a compass, and en route navigation aids were nonexistent. When the weather was good with adequate visibility, pilots used visual landmarks they could readily identify by peering out of the cockpit. A very common reference chart they would carry was a road map designed for automobiles. These maps identified not only the roads that existed at the time but also railroads, both of which the pilots commonly followed. However, these methods were acceptable only for daytime flying and were not adequate after dark – and they were totally useless in bad weather. If night flying or flying in marginal weather was ever to be achieved safely, alternative forms of navigation had to be found.

The stimulus for the development of reliable air navigation came when the airplane was recognized as an ideal platform for the rapid delivery of mail, and the airmail service began. However, reliable mail delivery required that it be delivered on schedule, and that requirement necessitated continuous flights during both day and night, regardless of weather.

The concept of airmail has been around since long before the invention of the airplane. Roman armies used carrier pigeons to send messages reporting their progress at the front. And pigeon-borne airmail continued for this purpose until well into World War I. On January 9, 1793, a personal letter from George Washington was carried by hot-air balloon from Philadelphia to Deptford, New Jersey, where the balloon ultimately touched down.[19] Washington had instructed the balloon pilot to deliver the letter to the property owner where the balloon landed. The letter would function both as an apology for the intrusion and as a commemoration of the first airmail delivery in the United States. But with the advent of the airplane, with its ability to take off and land at predetermined locations, the prospect of reliable airmail could now become a reality.

After several sporadic starts to establish airmail operations beginning as early as 1912, the world's first formally inaugurated airmail service began on May 15, 1918, when the US government initiated a scheduled route from Washington, DC, to Philadelphia and New York.[20] The plan was to make one round trip per day for six days a week. Because the country had recently entered World War I in Europe, the Aviation Section of the US Signal Corps was in need of pilots with more cross-country experience. Hence, the War Department had agreed with the Post Office Department that it would operate the airmail route for ninety days. At the time when the agreement was signed, however, there were no airplanes in the US inventory with sufficient range to make the 218-mile trip. The maximum range of the best existing airplane, the Curtiss JN-4D Jenny, was eighty-eight miles.

However, undeterred by any of this, orders were issued on May 6, 1918, to Major Reuben H. Fleet to modify the Jennies as necessary and have them capable and ready for an 11:00 a.m. departure on May 15. President Wilson would be present to witness the first takeoff. Major Fleet set about to convert six Jennies for this purpose. He had the standard ninety-horsepower engine replaced by the larger one hundred fifty-horsepower

---

[19] "Pass for Jean-Pierre Blanchard, 9 January 1793." Founders Online. National Historical Publications and Records Commission. https://founders.archives.gov/documents/Washington/05-11-02-0383.

[20] Wright, Nancy Allison. "The Reluctant Pioneer and Air Mail's Origin." 1999. http://www.airmailpioneers.org/content/milestone1.html.

engine; he modified the front seat of each into a compartment for carrying mailbags; and he doubled the fuel-tank capacities. After an intensive scramble with logistics and preparations, the assigned pilots and aircraft were finally in position for the main event.

The point of departure in Washington, DC, for the historic first flight was to be the Polo Grounds in Potomac Park, a fairly small, tree-lined, grassy area between the Potomac River and the Tidal Basin. The postal officials chose this location over the superior College Park, Maryland, airport as it was closer to the main post office. The pilot selected for this first flight, George Boyle, was essentially chosen as a political favor, as he was the future son-in-law of the then commissioner of interstate commerce. This selection was made over Major Fleet's objections, as Boyle was a very recent flight-school graduate with barely sixty hours of flying time.

As the departure hour approached on May 15, the mail truck arrived with four mailbags and a motorcycle escort. In the tradition set by George Washington, President Wilson placed into one of the opened mailbags a letter addressed to the New York City postmaster to commemorate the official first letter to be delivered by the newly formed airmail service. Boyle then climbed into the cockpit, and with the support of the ground crew, executed numerous unsuccessful attempts to start the engine. With all the pomp and confusion wrought with the initiation of the newly formed airmail service, no one had thought to fuel the airplane, and the actual takeoff was delayed by nearly an hour while mechanics scrambled to find gasoline. With the airplane finally fueled, a successful takeoff was executed, and the entourage disbanded and left the field.

Meanwhile, while the opening ceremony was taking place in Washington, DC, mail delivery flights had taken off from New York to Philadelphia and from Philadelphia to Washington, DC.

The pattern set up by Major Fleet was a circuit relay similar to that of the Pony Express, where the pilot from one location would land, transfer his mail to the aircraft of another pilot, who would then take off and fly the next leg to the next destination. The intent was that flights would be going in both directions. The mail from New York would land in Philadelphia and be transferred to the next aircraft along with the mail from Philadelphia and flown on to Washington, DC. Flights in the opposite direction would be occurring simultaneously. A window of time for transitions to take place was established.

Boyle didn't make it in time for his connection in Philadelphia, so the awaiting pilot left on schedule for New York without Boyle's mailbags with President Wilson's letter. As it turned out, Boyle became lost. Nearly out of fuel, he made an emergency landing in a field where he flipped his plane over and damaged the propeller. His mailbags were returned to Washington, DC, via truck.

Major Fleet objected to Boyle's further involvement because of his limited flying skills, but the postmaster general insisted that he be given another chance. Two days later Boyle was off again, and once more he became lost. Low on fuel, he landed in a field, bought more gasoline, and asked for directions to Philadelphia. However, upon arriving at Philadelphia, he was unable to find the designated airfield and again ran out of fuel, making an emergency landing on the Philadelphia Country Club golf course. This time, although unhurt, his aircraft was destroyed. Over protests from postal officials who wanted to give Boyle yet another chance, Major Fleet had him removed from service.

In spite of the rough start, the fledgling airmail service had a successful initiation and was supported by pilots from the Army Air Service until August 10, 1918, when the Post Office Department assumed operations. Although there were numerous forced landings due to bad weather or mechanical failures, the army pilots completed this mission without a single fatality.

With the success of this first experiment came the desire for even more airmail routes, which in turn applied ever greater pressure on the need for en route navigation systems. Since the expanded airmail operations would take place around the clock, it became imperative that supplemental navigational supports be implemented. One of the earliest and most obvious navigational aids was bonfires that were lit each evening by the post office staff and others along the route of flight. These rapidly evolved to artificial beacons placed on towers and hilltops, visible for several miles at night to guide pilots. By the early 1920s the idea was put forth to light the airport boundaries to make them more readily distinguishable to pilots. Lighted wind socks were quickly added, as were rotating beacons. The post office was instrumental in completing a transcontinental airway of beacons, and once these beacons were in place, regularly scheduled night operations began over part of this route.

In 1926 the Air Commerce Act created the Air Commerce Branch of the Department of Commerce. This new branch of the government would be responsible for pilot testing and licensing, aircraft certification, and accident investigations. The new department immediately assumed the responsibility for maintaining and expanding the lighted airways, and by 1933 it had lengthened the beaconed airways to over eighteen thousand miles. Furthermore, at this point new standards were being implemented for minimum runway lighting requirements and likewise for runway lengths themselves. Even prior to the transfer of responsibility from the post office to the Air Commerce Branch, the post office was beginning to focus its efforts more closely on safety and reliability, and this endeavor was continued and expanded by the Air Commerce Branch.

This new navigational system initiated by the post office and continued by the Air Commerce Branch was great when visibility was good, but what about periods when the weather was bad? How were pilots to know if they were flying into an area of clouds, especially at night? Pilots were able to get weather reports prior to takeoff, but they had no means of learning of changes while en route. The development of two-way communication technology was essential, and work had finally begun on this in December of 1926. Two years later, new radio stations were installed with the capability of sending voice communications as aids to navigation.

But a more reliable navigation system was still needed for foul weather, and in 1928 a radio beacon system was developed. A year later, a four-course radio range was standardized. With this system pilots could maintain their course by listening to audio signals. One half of the four-course signal would transmit the Morse code for the letter A, which is *dot dash*, and the other half would transmit the Morse code for the letter N, which is *dash dot*. Pilots would guide their airplanes along a course where they would hear a continuous tone. If they started to hear a *dash dot, dash dot*, they knew that they had been drifting too far to the right, for example, and would steer their airplanes slightly to the left until they picked up the continuous tone once more. If they heard a *dot dash, dot dash*, they would do the opposite. This technology continued to be used for civilian aircraft through World War II.

The instruments onboard the aircraft were also improved through the late 1920s. One significant addition to the instrument panel was the altimeter. Although the altimeter was invented in 1916, the first accurate barometric altimeter, capable of converting atmospheric pressure into altitude above sea level, didn't come into being until 1928. And the patent for the first reliable directional gyro, a more accurate means of determining heading than a compass of that era, was filed in 1931. The period from 1928 through 1931 was especially important for aviation, as it was during this period that new systems of navigational technology came into being, rendering long-distance flights safer and more reliable.

The addition of more accurate onboard instruments, coupled with the advent of more reliable radio navigational beacons, now opened the door for safer all-weather flying. Pilots would not necessarily be grounded due to the deterioration of visibility while en route. The first official test flight of this new instrument-only system was conducted by James "Jimmy" Doolittle on September 24, 1929,[21] who at the time was an army lieutenant. With these new instruments on board enabling him to know his aircraft's attitude, altitude, and heading without looking outside, he successfully took off, climbed to his assigned altitude, flew around for a bit, set his course for a return to the airport, and successfully landed, all with the use of the aircraft instruments alone.

The genie was now out of the bottle, and in the 1930s the technologies and flight adaptations for panel-mounted instruments, as well as both verbal and navigational communications, accelerated. But even then there was an excessive amount of missing information. Elevation information for terrain clearance was virtually nonexistent. Suggestions for the best routes to fly in mountainous regions were not available. Especially missing was information on the best approach pattern for pilots to follow for the safest alignment and descent into airports when descending through clouds. In 1930 a road map was still the only available aviation chart.

---

[21] Swops, Brian R. "24 September 1929." 2015. This Day in Aviation – Important Dates in Aviation History. https://www.thisdayinaviation.com/24-september-1929/.

The need for this additional information was an obvious concern for all pilots flying scheduled routes, and they shared everything they learned with one another, from best routes to fly to anomalies of specific aircraft. But in 1930 one pilot in particular, Elrey B. Jeppesen, who had hired on that year with Boeing Air Transport as a contract pilot for the post office department, did something about this issue.[22] His route was the mountainous region between Salt Lake City, Utah, and Cheyenne, Wyoming. He recalled during an interview many years later that, during the winter of 1930, four pilots were killed while flying the Cheyenne to Oakland, California, route. That was four of the eighteen pilots who had been assigned that route. He felt that the potential dangers were unacceptable, and for one dime he bought his now famous "little black notebook" and set about compiling information critical to the routes he was flying.

He initiated this task by land, driving over his assigned routes to quantify the terrain. He would climb mountains and record the altitudes, he took photographs, he wrote down suggested climb rates for his aircraft to ensure terrain clearance, he determined obstructions around airfields and ways of avoiding dangers in bad weather, he quantified details of the airfields he would be landing in, and he even obtained phone numbers of locals who could give him weather reports. Word got out among fellow pilots about his having obtained this information. At first he gave copies to anyone who asked, but fairly soon the demand became so great that he started selling them. In the following years as more navigation information became available, he would update his little black notebook with these revisions. In 1931, for example, low-frequency radio beacons became available, and he

---

[22] Dumovich, Eve. "The Early Adventures of Captain Jepp." August 2005. Boeing Frontiers. Volume 04, Issue 4. http://www.boeing.com/news/frontiers/archive/2005/august/i_history.html.

added information on how pilots could use this new navigational aid. He continued to improve his charts until they became the instrument flying standard for North America, the now famous Jepps Charts. He was a true aviation pioneer.

So like all things, the era of the lone pilot droning along in an open cockpit was coming to an end. Passing like a fading dream was the time when he would listen to the wind whistle through the wing struts and guywires as the rainy sleet bombarded the fuselage and deflected off the short windscreen. With his head shielded from the elements by his leather helmet buckled under his chin, his massive goggles would be pulled down over his eyes to protect them from the wind and the pelting rain. His heavy, fur-lined gloves kept his hands from freezing as he manipulated the stick between his knees while wiping the face of his compass. The epoch of these daring souls dressed in their sheepskin leather flight suits and peering over the edge of their open cockpits was slipping into memory.

But it's the memory of a glorious era, a time trapped within its own capsule, made permanent by its own deeds and rendered possible through the sheer courage of these brave young adventurers who dared make it happen. Theirs was to stay their course in the face of all odds and fulfill their task to successfully deliver their assigned cargo by the appointed hour. Many a time their aircraft would fail them and crash land somewhere along the route. And many a time these same pilots, suffering cuts and bruises, would climb out of their damaged airplanes only to immediately clamber back into anything available deemed flightworthy to continue their runs – never complaining, never faltering, always unyielding and resolute and selflessly determined, unconcerned for personal welfare. Such is the stuff of legends.

CHAPTER 7

... AND THERE I WAS

There's ice on the wings
    And the air's getting rough
And the engine's beginning to hack.

That lightning flash
    Lit up the panel
To show all the fuel we lack!

The vacuum pump's failed
    And the DG's adrift,
And the compass is now leaking oil!

The yoke's getting stiff
    And the rudder won't play,
And the winds are beginning to boil.

The plane's being tossed
    Like a badminton bird
By a force from the bowels of Hell!

The noise from the sleet
    Grates through the bones,
Curdling my nerves to gel.

The prop's straining hard
    From the ice on its edge
To carve out one more bite.

But the oil pressure's low
    And the engine sounds strange.
And something just doesn't feel right.

The airspeed's odd –
    I forgot pitot heat!
As if I weren't busy enough.

I try raising Center –
    What was that pop?
Now the air is really getting rough!

The radio's now gone –
    And the navs are all out!
Now what am I expected to do?

I guess it's about time
    To hit the reset –
And run this simulation anew!

There's an old saying in aviation that it is much better to be down here wishing you were up there than it is to be up there wishing you were down here. Flying is an unnatural environment for us Earth-based creatures. All of our evolutionary, biological sensors are designed to tell us our orientation relative to the ground. We know up from down and all the other related positions. But when flying an airplane, especially in instrument flight conditions, all of those Earth-derived indicators are meaningless. So when learning to fly, the vast majority of one's training is focused on "what to do if …"

In primary training we are taught to aviate, navigate, and communicate. The aviate part, believe it or not, is the easiest. Most trainees take their first solo flight before they have logged ten hours. When the instructors think the trainees are ready, they step out of the planes and tell the trainees to take it around the pattern two or three times. The trainees then taxi to the runway, take off fairly smoothly, climb out on the upwind leg, bank into the turn to crosswind, enter the downwind leg, bank into the base leg, and join the turn to final for landing. Maybe the landings aren't perfect, but they're okay. They then taxi back to the departure end of the runway for another takeoff. Or if the instructors have so authorized, they push the throttle full forward for a touch-and-go for the next trip around the pattern. The trainees demonstrate that they can competently handle the airplane in flight and safely bring it onto the runway for a landing.

Navigating is a bit more complicated, as now trainees must learn how to set and interpret the various navigational aids mounted in the aircraft instrument panel. But with the help of ground school and a little bit of practice, they will come to master that as well. They will soon be navigating from Point A to Point B with confidence.

Communicating, however, is another matter. One would think that communications would be very straightforward. But for some odd reason, this area seems to be the most difficult. The likely explanation is that communication in the aviation world is like a code. The phrases must be expressed in the correct order, they have to be terse, and they must be expressed with acceptable words. Unfamiliar terms or phrases must be avoided. When pilots are busy keeping their airplanes straight and level while trying to find Point B, they often find themselves tongue-tied when keying the microphone to respond to calls from flight controllers. It happens to everyone; it's happened to Penny and me. But that's part of the training.

In parallel with all of this, fledgling pilots are subjected to hours of ground school, where they learn not only the theoretical aspects of flight but also the necessary supporting knowledge like airport markings and aviation charts.

Meanwhile, all during the time our intrepid trainees are learning to aviate, navigate, and communicate, their flight instructors are introducing them to the various stages of what-if scenarios. And this, believe it or not, constitutes the majority of their training. Flying the airplane when everything is working perfectly is really quite easy. But what happens when something goes wrong? What does one do? How does one respond?

It's during this stage of their training that our fledgling aviators demonstrate whether they have the "right stuff." Very early in this phase instructors will initiate an engine-out scenario by pulling the throttle all the way back so that the engine is merely idling. In this configuration there is insufficient power being generated to maintain altitude. How do the new fledglings react to that event? What steps do they take to "restart" the engine? If the engine can't be restarted, what do they do next? If they have to make an emergency landing, how do they prepare for it? Where do they go? During our primary training, our instructor would actually shut the engine off. Restarting in this circumstance became a very real issue! Although it never happened with us, this practice has since been discontinued, as on rare occasions there have been instances where the engine could not be restarted and an actual emergency landing resulted.

For additional what-if training, instructors will take the airplane to a fairly high altitude and subject new students to "stalls." The stall speed of an airplane is the point where lift over the wing is lost and the aircraft can no longer remain airborne. If nothing is done to correct this situation, the airplane will crash. Much early training is spent on recognizing and avoiding this event. The higher altitude is chosen to give the student plenty of time to correct.

The two most dangerous times for an airplane to stall is during takeoff and during the approach for landing. If a stall happens during these phases of the flight, the airplane is still very close to the ground and may not have sufficient altitude to recover. So it's imperative that new students be able to recognize the onset of a stall and react immediately to recover from it.

Our fledgling aviators are also subjected to what are called unusual attitudes, where instructors put the airplane into an abnormal orientation, and the students must then very quickly decide what needs to be done to reposition the airplane into its straight and level attitude.

And the new pilots-to-be must undergo hours and hours of takeoffs and landings. As every experienced pilot knows, the execution of the last few seconds of a landing is an art form. It's not something that can be intellectualized. One may know every principle of *how* to do it, but actually doing it correctly is something else altogether. This takes practice. Why this is so becomes obvious when one thinks about it. The stall speed for a small trainer airplane like a Cessna 152 is about fifty miles per hour with flaps down. So in order to keep the speed at a safe margin while slowing down to land, new students must come "over the fence" (the outer perimeter of the airport) and approach the "numbers" (the compass direction painted on the landing end of the runway) at a speed of at least sixty miles per hour. The ideal landing touchdown is where the airplane stall speed is reached exactly when the wheels touch the runway. However, that rarely happens. Instead, the airplane typically contacts the runway at freeway speeds, and the wheels and landing gear absorb all the energy of our fledglings' imperfect landings. Then the students push the throttle in to go around the pattern and do it again. This process continues until they develop a feel for how to execute a good landing. But even with all of this training, they will occasionally be reminded that, as they progress well into an extensive flying career, not every landing will be perfect. Even the professionals have bad days. We all have been on commercial flights where, upon landing, we would swear that the pilot was Captain Kangaroo.

With all of these tasks accomplished, the instructors will then decide that the students are ready to do all of this on their own. The instructors sign them off for cross-country solos, and our fledglings are on their way. After a few more accumulated hours of logged flight time, they will take their check-rides with an FAA-designated flight examiner.

Once they earn their private-pilot licenses, they may decide to go on for an instrument rating, and then their training really begins. The poem "… And There I Was" is an example of the category of incidents they will now train for. Any one of those events could come about, and they could happen when least expected in the worst of conditions. And over their flying lifetimes, they are virtually certain to experience one or two of them. Ideally, however, they will not let them accumulate, as the poor, hapless pilot in our tale did. With options rapidly disappearing, as they were in our story, one should immediately seek the nearest airport and land. And he or she should not be embarrassed to declare an emergency, if necessary.

Penny and I have been fortunate in all of our years of flying never to have experienced any major in-flight emergencies. That's not to say, however, that there haven't been occasional glitches. On at least three occasions that I can immediately recall, we have lost the function of one cylinder due to a spark plug foul-up. And that's a significant power loss for a four-cylinder engine. Fortunately, in all three instances, we were near an airport where we could put down and have the problem corrected.

One of those incidents, however, was on a takeoff roll as we were leaving Deer Valley Airport outside of Phoenix. Penny was in the left seat for this one while I was looking out the side door window, staring at the passing runway, daydreaming. The plane was accelerating down the runway and had nearly obtained sufficient speed for liftoff when, suddenly, one cylinder started banging, creating a significant power loss. As I was being snapped out of my reverie, Penny had already pulled the power back and was slowing the plane down to exit the runway. Her reaction to this incident was so fast that she had the plane heading onto the taxiway before I even realized what had happened. She obviously knew "what to do if …"!

We have twice experienced total electrical failure while in flight, once as we were approaching our home airport and once when we were on an IFR flight plan. The electrical loss during the approach to our home airport was our very first experience like this, and that prompted us to have an additional gauge installed in the instrument panel to enable us to tell when the battery was discharging. Since the time of that installation, the warning emitted by that gauge has enabled us to return to our home airport on two other occasions before the battery itself died after loss of the generator output.

The power for the electrical system on our airplane, a 1967 Mooney Executive, is supplied by an onboard generator instead of an alternator. The generator delivers power to all activated systems, such as the radios and transponder, as well as keeping the battery charged. To accomplish this, the electricity produced by the generator is transmitted to the electrical system through brushes that ride in contact with a rotating shaft. But brushes wear down and require periodic replacement, so they must be inspected for wear during each annual maintenance cycle. However, this requirement is not always rigorously followed, and this step is occasionally missed, especially for an older airplane. That's basically what happened to cause our electrical failures. Newer aircraft models are typically powered by alternators that don't have this problem. The engine, of course, will continue to run even if all other electrical systems have failed because the engine's electrical source is from magnetos, which operate independently of the primary airplane electrical system.

But our primary training had prepared us for just such an occurrence. When our first electrical failure happened, we entered the pattern and rocked our wings to notify the tower that we had lost communications. This action informed the controllers that once we were on final approach, we were to receive landing instructions via lights that they would direct toward us – green, cleared to land; red, go around. As we entered the final leg, we saw the green light and continued our landing. Once on the ground, we called the tower and told them of our electrical failure and thanked them for the green light. Shortly thereafter, we bought a handheld navigation-communication, or "nav-com," radio for just such occurrences.

The electrical failure we experienced while on an IFR flight plan was somewhat different. We were returning home from Phoenix and were flying westbound in and out of clouds at eight thousand feet. As we approached the Colorado River, suddenly all of our electrical panel went blank. Fortunately, when that outage occurred, we were in a temporary clearing where we had good visibility, and we were fairly close to the Blythe, California, airport. We set the transponder code to 7600, indicating we had lost our radio communications, and attempted to reconnect with Los Angeles Center via our handheld radio. But the signal was too weak to establish contact, so we decided to land at Blythe to assess our situation. Once on the ground, we called Flight Service to inform them of our situation and to cancel our IFR flight plan. Fortunately, there was a mechanic on duty who was able to troubleshoot our condition. The cause of our loss of electrical power this time was a loose belt that drove the generator, causing it to stop rotating. The mechanic tightened the belt and charged the battery sufficiently for us to start the airplane, and we were back in the air.

Once in the air, we requested an IFR pop-up through Los Angeles Center to continue our trip. A pop-up is a pilot request for IFR traffic control services through a center or an approach control. The traffic controllers are not obligated to take us, but they almost always invariably do. They recognize that we would not be requesting these services unless we really needed them. We have made this request numerous times over the years when we flew into what we considered to be marginal conditions for visibility, and we have never been turned down. A classic case where this may be necessary is around sunset at times when the atmosphere is fairly hazy. Under those conditions the visible horizon essentially disappears, and instruments are necessary for the maintenance of positional reference. When encountering circumstances such as these, not having experience with instrument flight is potentially dangerous. It was essentially this situation that John F. Kennedy Jr. encountered when he plunged into the ocean off Martha's Vineyard.

But even with instrument flying experience and being on an active IFR flight plan, a situation can arise where even these assets are not entirely helpful. And that circumstance happened to us one time when we were on a westbound IFR flight approaching Santa Fe, New Mexico, where we had planned to land for a fuel stop. We were at twelve thousand feet cruising above a solid layer of clouds below us. The weather conditions at Santa Fe were clear with a fairly high ceiling, the ceiling being the bases of the clouds we would have to fly through. The cloud layer itself was no more than two thousand feet thick. We had just crossed the Anton Chico VOR navigational aid and turned toward Santa Fe when the air traffic controller gave us our initial descent instructions for landing.

As we started down, we immediately entered the cloud layer. Normally, this event is very routine and something one typically doesn't give a second thought. But this time was different. We were no sooner completely immersed in the cloud when we were suddenly hit with a load of rime ice. We had ice all over the windshield, on the leading edges of the wings, and on the leading edges of the propeller. And it covered us very suddenly.

All icing conditions are hazardous to aircraft, and these environments can occur when an aircraft enters a cloud of minute, supercooled water droplets. Pure, undisturbed water can exist as a liquid well below its freezing point – hence, the term *supercooled*. The disturbance of an arriving aircraft provides a nucleation site and causes these tiny water droplets to suddenly change phase and precipitate as a solid. And it occurs very quickly! Icing changes an aircraft's aerodynamics by disturbing the airflow and destroying lift, and without lift the airplane can no longer remain airborne. To make matters worse, our airplane was not equipped with deicing equipment.

Shortly after we were suddenly covered with ice, the air traffic controller came on the radio and offered us a vector directly to the Santa Fe airport. Since traffic was very light and visibility at the airport was good, this vector would expedite our approach to landing. Now we had a dilemma. We had so much ice on the windshield that we couldn't see out. But from the side window we could tell that we were now below the cloud base, and visibility was clear for what seemed like miles. We thought that if we had just a little more time, then the ice would start flaking off the windshield, allowing us to see to land. We keyed the radio and declined the direct vector. Instead, we asked for the full IFR published approach for the airport landing. For this request we would fly directly to the VOR, execute a procedure turn, realign back onto the VOR, and proceed on our approach to the runway. This would buy us quite a bit of time, as we were a couple of minutes from the VOR, and each leg of a procedure turn is about a minute. We thought that by the time we had gone through all of that and started our descent to the runway, the ice would have flaked off the windshield. We already were being hit by chunks of it coming off the propeller and hitting the airplane. Furthermore, this entire procedure is normally executed solely on instruments.

It worked! As we were going about the formal procedure, bits of ice started flaking off the windshield. We could tell from the side windows that the majority had already fallen off the leading edges of the wings. But as we did our final pass over the VOR to begin our descent to the runway, there was still a large glob of ice on the center part of the windshield, and we had to lean to the side to see directly ahead. But it was disappearing fairly rapidly. We slowed our airspeed to buy a little more time, and by the time we were within a quarter mile of the landing threshold, all the remaining ice had flaked off. We landed completely without incident.

These are but a few examples of our experiences with incidents that turned out to be fairly benign. But had we reacted otherwise, each one could have ended quite differently, as was the situation with our hapless aviator in the poem. Fortunately, he was in a simulator. But many aviation fatalities in real life result from pilots losing aircraft redundancy through the accumulation of seemingly minor failures, any one of which at the time didn't appear so bad. Or they end up in flight conditions that initially appear benign but suddenly become untenable. The accrual of these adverse conditions adds up to losses of options.

If a pilot ever found himself even partway into the predicament that our poor soul from the poem was, then he should immediately declare an emergency and land as soon as possible. Various aviation friends of ours have over the years told us stories of in-flight failures they have experienced that forced them to land. One friend, for example, had an oil line failure that caused oil to spray all over the windshield. He was on his final approach to land at an airfield at the time of the incident, and he was able to see through the side of the windshield sufficiently well to accomplish the landing. He landed without incident and immediately had the failed part repaired. Had this incident occurred somewhere during midflight, the oil loss could have threatened the engine integrity and caused engine failure, likely forcing him to put down somewhere that was less than optimal.

We had a very similar incident on one of our return trips from Mexico. We were a few miles south of Mexicali, where we had planned to land for fuel and to clear customs, when we noticed a faint smell of oil. All the gauge readings looked good and we would be landing in a few minutes, so we didn't think much more about it. We landed and taxied to the fuel island, and an attendant came out to pump fuel for us while we were still in the plane getting our paperwork together. I was in the left seat at the time, and he came around to the left of the fuselage and pointed to the cowling. He told us in broken English that we had a problem with our oil. I immediately got out of the plane and went around to look. Yes, we had a problem. Oil had sprayed all over the root of the leading edge of the left wing and along the left cowling. I quickly checked our oil level on the dipstick and found that we were down to barely two quarts remaining from an eight-quart capacity. I then took off the cowling and discovered that the source of the leak was one of the high-pressure oil lines that had been rubbing against the exhaust manifold. The engine vibration had worn a pinhole through the steel braiding of the hose, and oil had been squirting out. These hoses had been recently replaced prior to that trip and apparently had been routed too close to the exhaust manifold.

Our next stop after Mexicali was Calexico, where we would clear US customs, and it was about a ten-minute flight from Mexicali. So we decided to fill the oil reservoir and, while allowing the leak to continue, quickly leave for Calexico. Once there, we would have the hose replaced. We always carried spare quarts of oil for these trips and did have some on board. Unfortunately, we had only four quarts with us, but we added all four, giving us slightly under six quarts to get us to Calexico. We did a quick calculation of probable leak rate and decided that we could make it and still have oil left.

As one additional precaution, we switched pilots. Through some strange quirkiness, over our years of flying, we both have noticed that I seem to be able to spot airports from the air much quicker, and Calexico is a small general-aviation airport that's tucked away and sometimes difficult to see. We couldn't take any chance of missing it and flying around looking for it. While Penny was flying, I could concentrate on finding the airport. When we contacted the Mexicali tower, we told the controller of our situation and our intent. The controller asked us if we needed any additional assistance, but we told him that we should be fine.

We took off with a minimal engine run-up to shorten our total operating time. It was slightly overcast that day, which reduced shadow contrast and made distinguishing surface features a bit more difficult. But Penny held the heading that would take us to the vicinity of Calexico. As we approached the border, I spotted what looked to be the airport environment, and Penny turned toward it. Since Calexico was an uncontrolled airport, she announced our position to advise other aircraft that we were inbound for landing. Then she lined up and landed directly without executing a full pattern entry. She immediately taxied to customs and shut the engine down, and I quickly got out and rechecked the oil level. We had used two quarts of oil during that ten-minute flight. We then cleared through customs. It was there that we learned that the Mexicali controller had called to see if we had arrived safely. That was a very nice gesture.

After customs, we walked over to a repair shop we had spotted. We found a mechanic on duty and inquired whether he would be able to replace our leaking hose. He told us that he could easily make the replacement, but unfortunately he didn't have the correct size hose on hand and would have to get one from a repair facility at one of the adjacent airports. But he did say that he could have the job completed by the next morning.

With that bit of news, we found our way to the De Anza Hotel, where we had stayed on a previous flight to Calexico. It's an old hotel built in the Spanish style of Old Mexico, with sweeping arches and wrought-iron trim. Our room furnishings were a bit dated, and there was a long diagonal crack in an inner wall – almost imperceptible, but there. *That probably happened during the last earthquake*, I thought. But our stay was comfortable and quite fitting with the focus of our recent trip.

After breakfast, we returned to the airport to retrieve our repaired airplane and were on our way again by midmorning. We saved the old hose, cut out the section with the hole, and mounted it on a plaque as a souvenir of our near miss.

Two of our friends had separate incidents of landing gear failing to deploy as they were setting up to land. In both cases, the hydraulic landing gear for the aircraft was activated by a switch on the panel, and the gear-down position was indicated by green lights. In the first incident, the pilot had attempted to deploy the landing gear but did not see the green light come on. Since she was already in contact with the airport tower, she requested a flyby to have the tower controllers look at her plane's landing gear to see if they could determine its state. Only one wheel was down. She then told the tower she would leave the pattern to a safe area and try to deploy the gear manually. She was successful and returned to land.

The second incident occurred during a simulated IFR flight where the pilot was wearing a hood to restrict outside visibility and a safety pilot was riding with him to watch for traffic. It was the safety pilot who told me of this incident. He said that his friend was so familiar with his aircraft that after he threw the switch to activate the landing gear and did not see a green light, he immediately, without a second thought, reached under his seat and activated the manual crank that brought the gear down manually. There was never a hesitation or any ambiguity. The safety pilot was impressed, as the pilot had never mentioned that there was even a problem.

All the incidents in these examples were addressed immediately and not allowed to progress further. But not all pilots are so lucky. Near-catastrophic events often occur when a pilot has few options left and must react instantly. An off-field landing frequently results, and every pilot has undergone extensive training specifically designed to prepare for just such an eventuality. One hopes never to have to act on this training but must always be prepared for it. Very likely we would not be in a simulator if such an event ever were to happen.

CHAPTER 8

THE PERFECT PUTT

It was not an especially eventful day,
　　When flying that afternoon.

I could have been heading for Tampa Bay,
　　Or off to Saskatoon.

The air was smooth and the engine purred,
　　As the land beneath me hurled.

My thoughts were one with my gliding bird,
　　And all was right with the world.

Then a sudden shake of the cowling frame
　　Woke me from my dream.

The engine sound was not the same –
   In fact, it began to scream!

As I checked the gauges, it banged and bopped,
   And I heard the rumble grow.

With a shuddering *clunk*, the engine stopped,
   While I watched the propeller slow.

The engine sputtered, twice then thrice,
   As I struggled to restart.

Then oil spewed out and the prop froze still
   As also did my heart!

I caught a glimpse of a fairway ahead
   As I pulled the throttle back.

"I'll put it down past the end of the shed
   By that old caddy's shack."

The fairway was long and my glide was sound,
   Skimming onto the eighteenth green.

Three duffers who saw me dove to the ground
   Strewing clubs all over the scene.

When I came to a rest and the plane shuddered still
   And I breathed my first sigh of relief,

One old duffer then came up the hill
   And proceeded to give me some grief.

He picked up his club and threw me a glare
As though he would wield me a blow.

"You fly people think you can land anywhere!
You cost me this game, you know!

"Your tires hit my ball on its way to the pin,
Though I'm happy you saved your butt.

"My only complaint is next time you drop in,
Don't screw up my perfect putt!"

This poem was written as a bit of tongue-in-cheek. In its stanzas, our intrepid aviator ventures forth in the same manner as he has for every other flight he has ever made when, suddenly, something unexpected happens. An emergency! What now? In the event of an actual in-flight emergency where the aircraft can no longer maintain altitude and landing is inevitable, where would one consider putting down? The subtle message here, as it turns out, is that a golf course may be ideal. The fairways are long and typically clear of trees, and there usually are no overhead power lines to worry about becoming entangled in. Save for the occasional sand trap or undulating terrain, the selection of a golf course for an emergency landing makes perfect sense. As mentioned in chapter 6, one of the earliest emergency landings made at the onset of the fledgling air mail service was in 1918 on the Philadelphia Country Club golf course.

But if a golf course isn't available, landing on a road or street is always an option. The problem with that selection, however, is that one must be wary of the direction of automobile traffic and land with it, and one must be extremely cautious of nearby power lines. Overhead power and communication lines virtually always follow along roads, especially the secondary country roads. This practice has resulted principally as a means of easy access to the power lines from virtually anywhere for ease of repair. The good news, however, is that these wires and poles are normally found on only one side of the road. If an emergency landing is ever necessary and a road is the only option, then by all means the pilot must note which side of the road the power lines are on.

But while we are on this topic, the subject of emergency landings deserves a bit of expansion. It is after all one of the major issues covered in primary aviation training. To begin, emergency landings are typically classified in two different categories – precautionary landings and forced landings. A precautionary landing is one in which the pilot suspects that there is a problem developing, typically with the engine, and lands at the nearest convenient airport while the engine is still producing power. This enables the aircraft to get safely onto the ground before an actual emergency develops. The pilot may or may not declare an emergency for this circumstance.

Over our many years of flying, we have made several precautionary landings, usually the result of the engine developing a misfire, often due to fouled spark plugs. Fortunately, the majority have occurred near our home airport. But on two occasions we had to leave the airplane at a distant airport, find transportation home, and reverse the process to recover the plane after repair.

On one of those incidents we were returning home from Flagstaff, Arizona, and we had one passenger on board. Penny was in the left seat during this flight. Shortly after takeoff, we both sensed that the engine seemed not to be performing as it should. It was very subtle. Unless one were truly familiar with that particular airplane, one likely would never notice. As we flew along, nothing really changed, but there was still the gnawing feeling that something was wrong. Penny and I talked about it while trying not to alarm our passenger, who was not familiar with aviation. Our dialogue was virtually monosyllabic, as each of us implicitly knows what the other is thinking sufficiently well that additional words are not required.

"What do you think?" she asked, knowing that I sensed what she sensed.

"Yeah, I agree," I said.

"Keep the road in sight where we can, but stay on the airway?"

"We'd better."

All the gauges looked good, and we were holding speed and altitude with no special effort, but we each sensed that there was an anomaly that we couldn't quite identify.

Immediately after takeoff, Penny had contacted Albuquerque Center for flight following with our destination being El Monte, our home airport. It was our tradition that we would ask for flight following for every flight we made. When on flight following, we are given a discrete transponder code, which puts us in the system for air traffic control, offering an extra pair of eyes when looking for traffic. It's an additional safety feature, and the controllers are always willing to oblige. And in our specific case for this flight, it gave us an immediate position location in the event of an emergency. Our anticipated time en route was on the order of three hours, and we followed the airways meticulously – first to Drake VOR adjacent Prescott, Arizona, then on to Needles, Twentynine Palms, and Palm Springs. This route assured us that we would always be fairly close to an airport in the event a real emergency ensued. Meanwhile, all the other parameters appeared to be normal; it's just that something didn't seem right.

As we were approaching Palm Springs from the east, we received a weather outlook telling us that the entire Los Angeles Basin was IFR with a low cloud cover everywhere. Normally, this condition would be a nonissue. However, over the previous few months at the time of this flight, the IFR patterns for the Los Angeles airspace were being reconfigured, specifically in regard to its interface with El Monte. This issue had originated a few months earlier when a pilot on an IFR flight plan to El Monte executed a missed approach and wandered into an LAX approach pattern. When that occurred, the FAA suddenly stopped all IFR approaches into El Monte whenever actual IFR conditions existed, and they would continue to be disallowed until the airspace repatterning was finalized.

We had been out flying a few weeks earlier when this order was in effect and had experienced this temporary restriction firsthand. Prior to our return to El Monte, as we were flying in from the west on that flight, a ceiling had formed over the airport. Knowing that because of this interim restriction we would be unable to acquire an IFR approach into El Monte, we requested an IFR approach into Burbank, which is only a few miles west of El Monte. Once we were under the clouds and noted that visibility was good and the ceiling was fairly high, we canceled IFR, broke off the approach, and continued VFR to El Monte and landed. But in the air east of Palm Springs where we were that day of the anomaly, we were not sure if the IFR airspace issue had been settled.

I don't remember who brought the subject up first, but we were both thinking about it. What would happen if we weren't allowed a direct IFR approach into El Monte and had to divert to Burbank to get under the clouds? The many vectors we would receive would involve multiple changes to the engine RPM, and the anomaly we thought we were sensing may become something serious.

"El Monte's IFR," I said in a terse yet coded tone. We were still careful not to use phrases that might upset our passenger.

"I don't like it," she responded.

"Let's put down in Palm Springs," I suggested.

"Good idea," she agreed.

We decided at that point to tell our passenger of our concern and then told her that we were going to do a precautionary landing at Palm Springs. Since we were on flight following, we had already been transferred to Palm Springs Approach Control. So Penny called Palm Springs Approach and told the controller of our change of plans and of our desire to land at Palm Springs. She didn't say that we were doing this because we had a concern, as everything was still performing normally. The controller gave her a vector for landing on Runway 13L, gave her a new altitude to maintain, and then told her to switch to the Palm Springs tower frequency.

When Penny turned the plane to the new heading, she pulled the throttle back to start our descent. But as she was throttling back, we were met by an enormous backfire! This little surprise confirmed to us that we had made the right decision. We needed to get onto the ground as efficiently as possible while the engine was still generating power. There was no other traffic into Palm Springs at that time, so we entered the pattern on a right downwind leg. Penny did an outstanding job flying the landing approach. She held just enough power setting to keep the engine RPM up slightly to control our descent so as not to have to vary the throttle while setting up for landing. On short final, she then backed off the power and executed probably the most beautiful landing of her flying career. Once off the runway, we taxied to the general-aviation parking area, parked, and shut down the engine. Penny could then breathe. This was also the first time our passenger said anything since the backfiring.

When we checked in at the general-aviation office, we were told that because it was Sunday there was no mechanic on hand, but he would be available in the morning to troubleshoot the problem. This option was fine with us, as the airplane wasn't going anywhere until a competent mechanic looked at it. From there, we went directly to the rental car counter to arrange transportation for the last leg of our trip home.

The following afternoon we called the general-aviation maintenance office to learn if there had been a diagnosis. Indeed there had been, confirming to us that our precautionary landing was a very wise decision. It turned out that the problem was with one of the magnetos, specifically its attachment to the engine block. The magnetos, which supply electric current to the spark plugs, are bolted to the engine with two bolts, each bolt passing through a protruding tab from the magneto housing. There apparently had been a flaw in the casting of the metal housing of one of ours, as the combination of required bolt torque and engine vibration had caused one of those tabs to completely fail and the remaining tab was severely cracked. This magneto was loose, causing it to intermittently discharge incorrectly and thus disrupting the timing of the spark plug firing, which affected the engine performance and explained the anomaly we had sensed.

Everything about airplanes involves redundancy. For our class of airplane, each cylinder has two spark plugs, and there are two magnetos that fire the plugs. Each magneto is connected to only one of these plugs per cylinder so that the failure of one magneto does not precipitate a total engine failure. During the run-up prior to every takeoff, the integrity of each magneto is individually checked with the engine ignition. Our run-up in Flagstaff didn't reveal any anomaly.

A few days later our friends Dave and Coleen Campbell volunteered to fly us over to Palm Springs so that we could settle the bill and pick up the Mooney. While there, the mechanic showed the four of us the failed part – the broken tab. The remaining severely cracked tab was not going to survive much longer. Our precautionary landing into Palm Springs had been a very wise decision. Had we decided to continue onward for an IFR approach to either El Monte or Burbank, the vibration that would likely have resulted from multiple engine RPM changes could have easily caused the second tab to fail also. I shudder to think of the consequence of the second one failing and the entire magneto coming loose while in flight. The universe was kind to us, and we were forgiven this time!

The second category of emergency landings is forced landings. A concept that instructors instill into their students during primary training is that a forced landing is a controlled crash. And surviving this controlled crash depends upon how well it's controlled. The slower one impacts, the better. The ideal state is to be hanging right at stall speed at the point of impact. Murphy's Law will ensure that a perfect touchdown zone will not be available. Instead, the pilot should seek a clear approach zone and focus on maintaining control of the aircraft while avoiding abrupt maneuvers and steep turns.

One of the more common and often fatal forced landings is the result of engine failure immediately after takeoff. The airplane typically is no more than a few hundred feet off the ground, and pilots inevitably attempt to return to the airport instead of landing straight ahead. Most never make it. Everyone who owns an airplane needs to know the minimum altitude loss expected for that airplane to return to the airport in the event of an engine-out on takeoff, and for single-runway airports that includes a short procedure turn to enable the aircraft to properly align with the runway. We practiced that maneuver with our Mooney. We would climb to several thousand feet to allow for plenty of margin and practice with both gear up and gear down. We found that we would have a difficult time completely turning around with less than a five hundred-foot altitude loss. A seven hundred-foot margin would be a lot better. So we always kept in the back of our minds that if we lost power on takeoff at altitudes less than these numbers, we would land straight ahead.

The problem arising from that constraint is determining what actually lies straight ahead. For our home airport, this was not an issue. It has a river wash that runs parallel to the runway, and the wash has a concrete surface that offers a nearly ideal emergency landing site. Over the decades that we have been based at that airport, we have heard of occasional times when emergency landings have been made in the wash. In fact, one occurred immediately in front of us on one occasion as we were approaching the runway shortly after we had called in for landing. The pilot involved had been cleared for takeoff prior to our arrival but lost engine power on the climb-out. He immediately told the tower he was putting it down in the wash. By the time our wheels were touching down, he called the tower again to say that he was fine but the aircraft had some damage.

Possibly purely for self-defense, we had adopted a special safety awareness technique when at airports other than our home airport. Very early in our flying career, we developed the habit of noticing environments at runway ends just as the wheels started to lift off its surface and we began to see a little farther ahead. A surprisingly large number of general-aviation airports do have an end zone where one very likely could survive an engine-out emergency landing. However, there are also many airports that are much less emergency-friendly, and Murphy's Law again says the engine-out experience will occur at one of those.

But if a forced landing is inevitable and a pilot has no other options, then ideally he or she should look for an open area and as smooth a surface as possible. A road, as we discussed above, is always good. An open field works. But even with an open field, terrain surface is not always known. For aircraft with fixed landing gear, there is no alternative. But for airplanes with retractable gear, there is a running debate as to whether it's better to land with gear up or gear down. There's an advantage to gear down, as the landing gear can absorb much of the impact energy, even if the struts fail. But if the surface is too rough, the airplane could flip over on impact, causing even greater injury to the occupants. For forced landings on soft surfaces and on water, the general consensus is that the landing should be made gear up. Ditching in water is much more complicated. Not only is wind direction important, but also the pilot must determine the direction of the swells and try to land parallel to them if possible. Also, for very rough surfaces, one might consider a gear-up landing there as well. As long as one bears in mind that the objective is to keep the cockpit and its occupants intact at the expense of the remainder of the airframe, one has a good chance of surviving a forced landing. The airframe is expendable, and a shearing wing absorbs a lot of energy. Treetops help absorb energy. Catching the airframe in a fence also works. There's not much time to think about options, so every pilot should have practiced what-ifs so as to have in mind what he or she would most likely do.

We have been very fortunate in our flying career. In our more than three decades of involvement in general aviation, we never have had to make an emergency, off-field, forced landing. However, in two instances, we were likely within minutes of such need were it not for the fact we had already landed, only to then discover that we had a problem. The first instance happened fairly shortly after we bought our Mooney and had been flying it for only a few years. Early in our ownership of it, we had decided to at least once have its annual inspection done by an organization that specializes in Mooneys. The logic for this was that, as a specialist, such an organization might catch subtleties specific to our make and model of airplane that a more generic inspection station might miss. So we had arranged that year to have its annual performed at one of these locations.

Shortly after we picked the plane up from the inspection station, we left on a cross-country trip to Vermont. Our planned fuel stop for the first leg of that trip was at Love Field in Prescott, Arizona, approximately a two-and-a-half-hour flight from our home airport. Penny was in the left seat on this leg. Once she had leveled off and trimmed the plane for our cruise altitude, she continued to adjust the fuel-leaning settings, stopping at the optimum cylinder-head temperature. When she finished verifying that all the readings were where they were supposed to be, I noticed that the fuel-mixture knob was not as far out as it typically should be for the altitude we were flying. I played with the knob for a while to see if maybe somehow it had become readjusted. But then I noted that if it were positioned to where it normally would be, the cylinder-head temperatures would be excessive. I thought that was odd, but all the other parameters were normal. We continued on to Prescott, landed, and taxied to the fuel island.

When we got out of the plane and walked toward the fuel pumps, we both noticed that the entire left side of the front cowling was covered with a blue film. We had a massive fuel leak! Aircraft fuel is color-coded, and there's a blue dye put into 100-octane avgas (aviation gasoline). We had to do something immediately. Penny went to the maintenance shop that happened to be close by while I proceeded to remove the cowling. I had just finished taking off the last section of cowling when she returned with a mechanic. When we all looked at the engine, we could see that the problem was obvious. The area around one of the injectors was saturated in blue. The mechanic reached for the injector – and it came off in his hand! He swore, making a cryptic comment about incompetent maintenance. Then he immediately retracted his statement, saying that possibly the mechanic who installed the injector had been distracted. Then he told us that because there was less than one thread holding the injector, had we flown much longer – possibly on the order of minutes – the injector likely would have fallen out, and we would have been looking for an off-field place to land. While he was checking and retorqueing all the remaining injectors, he found two others that were very loose. We were lucky. And that explained the anomaly I had noticed in flight with the position of the fuel-mixture knob.

We had a follow-up issue that related to this incident. Toward the end of our next leg, which was to Liberal, Kansas, I noticed the oil pressure gauge suddenly drop to zero as I had just finished setting up for landing. That was not good! But none of the other parameters, specifically temperatures, had changed. We completed our landing, taxied to parking, and immediately shut down the engine. I had suspected that because of possible excess heat generated from the earlier incident at Prescott, some of the oil could have been pyrolyzed and gummed up the gauge – or we had a major problem. It was early afternoon on a Sunday and not much was happening at the airport. We were concerned that we may be forced to spend the night in Liberal until Monday morning, when we could find a mechanic to assess this problem. Then we noticed a nearby hangar door open and walked over to it.

Once again, luck was with us. Two mechanics were changing out the engines on a twin, and one of them was working on something on a bench. We asked him if he could look at our oil-pressure gauge, which he did. He had us start the engine, and he didn't hear or see anything abnormal, except the gauge didn't move. We told him of our earlier incident that day, and he too suspected contamination in the gauge. He said he could remove the gauge and clean it, which would only take a few minutes, and that could be all that was needed. Then he continued to tell us that if, after reinstalling the gauge, the oil pressure didn't change, then we had a major problem and would have to leave the plane for at least a day. There was not much we could do, so we asked him to clean it and see what happened. Again we lucked out. The problem was only a contaminated gauge, and we were fueled and back in the air within the hour.

When this trip was over and we related this incident to our fellow pilots, the more experienced ones told us that there is an unwritten rule among aviators: never plan a long trip immediately following an annual inspection. Regardless of the competence of the shop doing the work, one is always a test pilot on that first flight when the plane is returned from its annual. That was a lesson well learned.

The second incident was more subtle and fell under the general category of "all for the want of a horseshoe nail." It happened at our home airport. We hadn't flown for a while and were doing a few touch-and-goes. I was in the left seat. I had originally planned to do eight touch-and-goes that day, but on the downwind of the sixth, I mentioned to Penny that I was happy with what I had done and suggested that we stop at this point and change pilots. With that, I turned base and backed off a little on power. I then turned final and backed off a little more. And on short final, I backed the power off to the point that the engine was barely above idle in preparation for touchdown. We touched down normally. But when I went to add a little power to taxi off the active runway, nothing happened! I had no control over the engine. Fortunately, I had enough forward momentum that I was able to successfully taxi off the runway and almost completely to the fuel island before coming to a full stop. At this point we had no idea what the problem was, save for the fact that we had no means of controlling the engine RPM. We called for assistance from ground operations, explained our situation, and requested a tow to parking. Once parked, we stopped by the local maintenance shop and asked if someone could assess the situation. We were advised that there was a job ahead of us, but someone would check it out in a day or so.

A few days later we received a call from the maintenance shop telling us what the problem was. There is a very small bracket bolted to the underside of the engine that the throttle cable passes through. The bracket stabilizes and guides the throttle cable. Unfortunately, it's in a very inconvenient location and often gets missed during inspections. The two bolts holding the bracket had backed out due to the engine vibrations, freeing the cable. With no guide bracket, the cable was useless. A major disaster could have resulted from the loss of what turned out to be virtually a five-dollar part. Again, the Fates were kind to us.

As our poem suggests, our fearless aviator left his home airfield without a care in the world, off to explore his universe by air, merely cruising along with his daydreams when his reverie was suddenly and abruptly interrupted. We all hope this never happens to us, but once our wheels leave the hard asphalt of the runway, all pilots are subliminally aware that the possibility, however remote, does exist. Most of us don't consciously think about it, but the impression is always there in the background.

But airplanes, for all of their frailties, are surprisingly resilient. Their designs are all about redundancy, and their structures are remarkably robust. So for the vast majority of our normal flying, we will be well within the envelope of safe operation. And statistically, our valiant aviator is much safer flying around in his airplane than he is driving back and forth between home and the airport. So climb into that cockpit, yell "Clear!" and fire up the engine. It's time to get a little air one more time. Being grounded is no condition for a Sky Walker.

CHAPTER 9

THE LURE OF THE LAST GREAT FRONTIER

No! There's the land. (Have you seen it?)
It's the cussedest land that I know,
From the big, dizzy mountains that screen it
To the deep, deathline valleys below.
Some say God was tired when He made it;
Some say it's a fine land to shun;
Maybe; but there's some as would trade it
For no land on earth – and I'm one.

There's a land where the mountains are nameless,
And the rivers all run God knows where;
There are lives that are erring and aimless,
And deaths that just hang by a hair;
There are hardships that nobody reckons;

There are valleys unpeopled and still;
There's a land – oh, it beckons and beckons,
And I want to go back – and I will.

I didn't write this poem. It was written in 1907 by Robert Service, the Bard of the North, whose most famous work is almost certainly "The Cremation of Sam Magee." These two stanzas were taken from his poem "The Spell of the Yukon." They, in my opinion, epitomize the magnificent vastness and starkness – and the severe beauty – of the extreme northern regions of the North American continent. And we flew over a large segment of this territory.

Of our more than three decades of flying all over North America, I can comfortably say that our greatest adventure was our flight to Alaska. This trip offered everything that one could hope for in a venture of this nature. It was long, lasting three weeks; it was virtually all flying, accumulating over fifty hours in the air; it involved all weather conditions, including many days of low ceilings; and it covered unfamiliar landscapes, requiring pilotage along rivers and through canyons. It challenged us with everything we had ever learned or experienced in the realm of aviation. Four of us made this trip together as a flight of two Mooneys, Gordon and Shirley Hughes in their Mooney and Penny and me in ours. All four of us were instrument-rated private pilots, so our expected encounters with inclement weather didn't especially concern us. We were prepared for that. For this trip we were exploring the unknown – unknown at least to us. We would loosely plan each day's route and destination and have cameras ready for any outstanding scenery or unforeseen events that may arise. Not only did we take a profusion of photographs to document this adventure, but I also kept a daily log.

Penny and I departed El Monte Airport in the late morning of Sunday, August 2, 1992, with a fairly heavily loaded airplane. We had removed the back seats to allow more room for equipment and supplies. Whenever one flies into northern Canada or Alaska, one is required by law to carry aboard specific provisions for survival in the event of a forced landing somewhere in the wilderness. There is a standard checklist for what these items must be, including firearms with ammunition. In addition to these items we also had camping equipment, food, and several days of clothes. All in all, we likely had the equivalent of at least one additional person in weight.

We had great visibility and smooth air as we headed up the San Joaquin Valley, California's primary agricultural area, on the day of our departure. We made a fuel stop in Modesto to change pilots before continuing on to Trinity Center, where we stopped for the night at the Airporter and Resort Inn, a place we had stayed the previous September. Our destination the following day was Bellingham, Washington, with a fuel stop in Eugene, Oregon. The weather again cooperated, remaining clear for this entire segment.

We arrived in Bellingham in the late afternoon. We gassed up and parked the plane, then checked into a motel to plan for our border crossing in the morning. We arranged to meet with Gordon and Shirley at the Transport Canada office of the Vancouver Airport, which was adjacent to the customs office. Since they were arriving from San Jose, this would be the first opportunity for the four of us to join up. From that point forward we would travel as a flight of two Mooneys.

Our first bit of news was regarding the weather forecast for the next day. The prediction was for overcast skies and possible rain in the morning. And indeed that was the case. When we arose at six that morning, the weather outside was solid IFR. Upon arriving at the Bellingham Airport to prepare for our departure, we learned that the reported ceiling was seven hundred feet and overcast, although Vancouver was reporting higher and broken. We departed Bellingham for our border crossing on an IFR flight plan.

After we crossed into Canada and made contact with Vancouver Approach Control, we were instructed to expect Runway 12 for landing. However, after we were already set up to land on Runway 12, the controller diverted us to Runway 8. Since we were still in the clouds at that time, we couldn't visually identify Runway 8. So we did a mad scramble to dial in the new instrument landing system, or ILS, frequency for that runway and turned toward it. Penny, who was in the left seat at the time, did a flawless IFR approach and landing into Vancouver.

After leaving the active runway, we taxied to the customs ramp. Until this specific trip, our only border-crossing customs experience had been in Mexico, where we typically had encountered multiple processing stations. The customs experience in Vancouver was just the opposite. We merely filled out one short form, and the customs agent was extremely polite.

We then caught up with Gordon and Shirley at the Transport Canada office. Gordon told us he had learned from flight service that there were widespread thunderstorms throughout the area we planned to fly through but the weather was expected to improve. After talking among ourselves, we decided to postpone continuing our trip by one day and instead stay the night in Vancouver. We then taxied to the Hudson General FBO for overnight parking and arranged for a hotel and rental car. With the extra time that had become available to us, we decided to drive to Whistler and check it out as a possible destination for the coming ski season. During the day while we were out exploring, the ceiling did rise and the clouds started to break.

We were finally on our way the next morning. As was predicted, the ceiling was indeed higher, at thirty-five hundred feet. But it was still overcast, although there were no expected thunderstorms. Furthermore, the weather was predicted to clear in central British Columbia. Our destination for the day was Watson Lake, a town in southern Yukon, with a stop at Prince George for lunch and fuel. But in the event that the clearing didn't occur as forecast, we filed an IFR flight plan to Fort St. John, a town farther north of our hoped-for fuel stop. The Prince George airport didn't have an IFR landing procedure. If the weather did clear as predicted, then we would cancel IFR and continue to Prince George, our preferred stop.

We climbed out of Vancouver on an IFR flight plan, heading eastbound along the airway toward the town of Hope. When we broke out of the cloud layer, we noticed that the cloud tops were at eighty-five hundred feet with solid overcast below us as we continued our climb. At Hope we turned north and followed our first-ever nondirectional beacon, or NDB, airway to Ashcroft, Williams Lake, and on to Prince George. The clouds became broken around Ashcroft, and by Williams Lake, the visibility was VFR. We canceled IFR about thirty-five miles out of Prince George as planned and landed there for fuel and lunch.

We had two options of navigation to Watson Lake. We could stay on the airway that took us east over Fort St. John, or we could go up the Trench, which would take us over Williston Lake. Williston Lake, though technically a reservoir, is the largest lake in British Columbia. Formed in a fairly narrow valley, it's only 96 miles wide at its widest point but is 156 miles long. We opted to fly up the Trench as the more adventurous option and took off VFR, climbing to sixty-five hundred feet. Because of the remoteness of this location and the lack of formal air services along this route, we were required to make occasional position reports at predetermined geographic points along the way. With the very good visibility we were experiencing, we had no problem identifying the reporting points.

It was a spectacular flight along Williston Lake and over wilderness that seemed to be as far removed from civilization as one could get. Although we remained at sixty-five hundred feet for the entire flight, the mountain peaks around us were higher and barren at the tops, and many still had patches of snow covering parts. Two forest fires were burning west of us along the way. This leg took us a little over three hours of flight time, which we flew entirely by pilotage over the lake. There were no navigational aids available along our route. Scattered-to-broken clouds began appearing midway along our route, but their bottoms were well above us. We picked up the airport VOR for Watson Lake around forty miles out, followed it inbound, landed, fueled, and got a motel for the night. We were delighted with our decision to fly up the Trench.

The weather the following morning was what we would come to call Alaskan VFR. The skies were overcast and drizzly, the aftermath of a late-night thunderstorm that had passed through. We learned from our weather briefing that the clouds were scattered to broken with bottoms around five thousand feet, and conditions were improving west of us, the direction we were heading. The visibility was fairly good. We talked with a pilot who had just landed from the west, and he told us that the worst of the "scuddiness" was between Watson Lake and Whitehorse.

We took off westbound from Watson Lake, climbed to forty-five hundred feet, and followed the Alaska Highway, a very long emergency runway. In fact, road signs along it alert drivers: "Caution: Landing Aircraft." The road wended through a narrow canyon with mountaintops of five to six thousand feet. The scud looked thicker as we approached each bend, but as we entered the curve, it would seem to break and visibility improved. We were rained on occasionally, but clouds were never worse than scattered, save for the overcast above us.

At this point, allow me to elaborate a bit on what I mean by *Alaskan VFR*. Until we made this trip, the vast majority of our flight altitudes typically had been fairly high. Altitude brings with it an inherent safety and sense of security. Not only do we have terrain clearance, but we also have relatively long glide distances in the event of engine failure. When one considers that the surface elevation of the Watson Lake airport is around twenty-two hundred feet, a flight altitude of forty-five hundred feet is not very high above ground level, especially with the nearby mountain peaks above us. Even though we were following a fairly flat road with no obvious hills and flight visibility was fairly good, being only twenty-three hundred feet above the ground at first made us feel a bit uncomfortable. But then as we were approaching Whitehorse, we saw another aircraft flying at a significantly lower altitude below us. Gordon was first to spot the other airplane and brought it to our attention over the radio on our preselected, unused frequency. We discussed the altitude of the other aircraft and noted that with the months-long prevailing overcast in this part of the world, maybe that's the way of life for local aviators. Visibility below the clouds is generally very good, but the clouds are often quite low. However, the freezing-level altitudes even in the summer are also typically relatively low, rendering IFR flights potentially hazardous for aircraft without deicing equipment. So to fly in this part of the world, we noted, we likely would virtually always be at a low altitude. We concluded this discussion with the observation that there is VFR as we know it, and then there's Alaskan VFR. This terminology stuck with us for the remainder of our trip.

We landed at Northway, Alaska, where we went through US customs, as we were now back in the States. The customs official was a real character, and we knew his entire life history by the time we cleared through. For example, he goes south for the winter – to Montana. He also asked us if we had any firearms on board. We told him that indeed we did, as it's required by law. He laughed at the response and told us that this was his trick question.

After lunch we took off from Northway for Fairbanks, again following the Alaska Highway. The valley widened, displaying a profusion of sodden marshes and countless small ponds, streams, and rivulets. The weather improved to scattered cumulus clouds, but the air became a little turbulent, giving us a bit of a bumpy ride all the way to Fairbanks.

We arrived at the Fairbanks International Airport without incident and arranged for parking our airplanes for the next couple of days. We rented a car at the airport and headed into town to find a place to stay. As luck would have it, all the hotels in Fairbanks were booked. Being the middle of the summer, several events were occurring at the same time, not the least of which was the beginning of the county fair starting the day after we arrived. But we found a very nice bed and breakfast where the owners were very accommodating. This being our first experience so far north in the summer, we were not paying attention to the actual time and got to bed very late. The sun was still above the horizon at ten o'clock, and by eleven thirty it was only dusk.

We had planned to spend a couple of days in Fairbanks exploring the general area, with our ultimate objective of scheduling a tour of Denali Park. The next morning we focused our attention on Denali and arranged for a park tour that would begin around three in the afternoon on Sunday, two days later. To ensure that we would have accommodations for an overnight at Denali, we had reserved a two-bedroom cabin in nearby Healy some five months in advance of this trip. A Sunday tour was important to our schedule to fit with our prearranged overnight room reservations at the Sourdough Inn in Healy for that day. The weather around Fairbanks was beginning to deteriorate to a condition of low ceiling with about a two-mile visibility; so not knowing what the weather might be by Sunday, we decided to remove any weather-related concern and drive to Denali. There was a runway adjacent to the park, but there was no instrument approach for it.

Since we were going to be spending a couple of days in Fairbanks, we checked around to see what activities were being suggested as points of interest that we might want to explore. We learned that there was a riverboat tour of the Tanana River being offered aboard a paddle wheeler and decided we would do that. But before the tour began, we returned to our airplanes to get our winter clothes we had left there when we arrived. Although it was warm when we arrived, the prevalence of overcast skies with temperatures in the low fifties made the air feel rather cold.

As we were closing the aircraft doors, we noticed the very large tires installed on an airplane parked fairly close to ours. Its pilot was packing something into the plane, so we walked over to ask about this seemingly unusual configuration. I don't remember the exact model of the airplane, but it was possibly a Maule. It was a fairly large single-engine tail-dragger with a three-bladed propeller. Its tires looked like balloons. They were nearly three feet in diameter and were smooth, with no tread at all. And they seemed fairly soft. When we asked the owner about them, we told him that we had just arrived and had never seen tires like these before. He laughed and said that these were tundra tires. They are large tires inflated to low pressures that allow flight operations on rough terrain and even limited operation on swampy land and directly on water when the aircraft is moving. These tires provide much greater cushioning and enable pilots to land on surfaces unsuitable for normal tires. He told us that he was a bush pilot and found these tires invaluable. He has landed and taken off from river banks, using the river itself as part of his makeshift runway. He indicated that we would be seeing many more of these as our trip continued, and he was right.

We then noticed the propeller on his airplane, or more specifically its leading edges. It was unbelievably pitted and hammered. Pieces even appeared to be missing. We asked him about that also. He replied that the terrain he lands on is brutal and known for throwing up debris, and he has to have the propeller refurbished periodically. This one was about due.

We thanked him for his enlightening input and returned to the car. We then drove to the Tanana River dock, where we joined the Discovery III paddle wheeler for the riverboat tour. Among the highlights pointed out along the river were the salmon traps used in years past by the Athabaskans, the indigenous people of the area. We also stopped at a simulated Eskimo village and received a most informative lecture on sled dogs. These were working sled dogs that participate in the annual Iditarod Trail Sled Dog Race. The air temperature remained fairly cool all throughout this tour, and we were very happy that we had retrieved our jackets.

The following day was dedicated to exploration. After a leisurely breakfast, we visited the Museum of the North at the University of Alaska. Although small, it presented an impressive theme of the cultures, artifacts, history, and animals indigenous to Alaska. By the time we finished the museum visit, the ceiling was lifting, so we decided to check out the Tanana Valley Fair. For me this was a very nostalgic experience, reminiscent of years gone by. What we found was a quaint little county fair with all the 4-H and Future Farmers of America kids and their livestock on show. We wandered around all the booths, petted the livestock, admired the arts and crafts, listened to some country music, and had a marvelously good time.

The evening's salmon dinner finished off a most pleasant day. We turned in a bit earlier that night in preparation for our planned drive to Denali the next day.

After a fairly early breakfast the next morning, we were on the road for Denali. Ours was a wise decision to drive, as the ceiling at the Fairbanks airport was reported at 500 feet scattered to broken, with measured 1,330 feet overcast. We even drove through patches of fog on the way to the park. However, the ceiling did began to rise as we approached Denali.

As soon as we arrived, we located the visitor desk at the Denali Hotel and picked up our tour tickets that we had bought in Fairbanks. From there we walked over to the landing strip and looked at the runway. It was a packed dirt runway that we could have easily negotiated in VFR conditions. But with a low ceiling and no provision for an IFR landing, driving was much smarter. After that, we drove to the Sourdough Inn to check into our cabin.

We returned to the park entrance, had lunch, and waited for our afternoon tour departure. The entire trip around the park would take over seven hours. While billed as primarily a wildlife viewing tour, where we saw moose, caribou, three grizzly bears, and Dall sheep, an unexpected bonus of this tour was the fantastic scenery. Retreating glaciers were dispersed sporadically along the sides of the mountain, exposing crumbling gray rock outcroppings jutting from their edges. The many streams of glacial flour – the silt left by the grinding rock from melting glaciers – would merge with the freshwater streams and flow unmixed for what seemed like miles. What we saw was what one might imagine the sights would have been at the end of the Ice Age.

Because of the long August days, the sun was still up when the tour ended around nine in the evening. We climbed down from the bus, walked to where our car was parked, and drove to our motel in Healy for the night. We planned to return to the park in the morning to drive around it ourselves before heading back to Fairbanks.

The morning found the weather to be clearing, and we felt that our chances were fairly good that we would get some good photos of Denali. On our way into the park, we were treated to two caribou walking along the centerline of the road. We stopped and got their photos. By then the clouds were breaking up, and visibility was becoming quite extensive, enabling us to get some excellent shots of the mountain itself.

By midmorning we decided to drive back to Fairbanks, arriving there shortly after noon. The skies at Fairbanks were clear, sufficiently so that we decided to fly to Anchorage that afternoon; and while on our way, we would take a short detour over Denali to inspect the mountain from the air. And we would fly VFR even though there were reports of a forty-five-hundred-foot broken ceiling beginning at Healy and extending to points south. When we did take off a couple of hours later, we were faced with a thirty-knot headwind and some turbulence. We climbed to thirty-five hundred feet for this flight – high by Alaskan standards! We were still having difficulty adjusting to this mind-set. We then headed straight to Healy where we would go through Windy Pass, which it was.

As we neared Healy, we turned right toward Denali with the intent of flying around the mountain itself, if the clouds had cleared from it. The ceiling in the immediate vicinity of the mountain was considerably higher than that reported near Healy, but Denali's back side was totally obscured. So we settled for attempting a flyby near the surface at its higher elevations. We had spotted a herd of Dall sheep partway up the mountain that we thought would make a great photograph. However, mountains make their own weather, especially peaks like Denali that tower well above and are isolated from other mountains. The air was slightly turbulent as we started our little detour, and as we got closer to the mountain itself, the turbulence increased to the point that it became moderate to severe. We were getting hammered! The mountain was trying to tell us that we were close enough, and we took its word for it and turned away.

As we turned east to follow the main road south of Healy that would lead us into Anchorage, we noted that the forty-five-hundred-foot broken ceiling reported earlier had now become overcast. Furthermore, the ceiling was a bit lower than reported and was coming down. We descended to get under the clouds and stay over the road, Alaska Route 3, for the remainder of our flight. We joined the road near where it was entering a pass, and the cloud edges on each side of the pass were flowing down the hillsides on either side, forming vortices that curled upward on each side of the road. They looked like rotor clouds. It was a breathtaking sight, but it was also a warning to prepare for more turbulence. We were not disappointed.

Route 3 follows the Susitna River for the majority of its extent but departs from it near the town of Willow, where the road continues eastward on to Anchorage and the river flows south into the Cook Inlet. We stayed over the road for the remainder of our flight, but the river was visible to us until the road departed from it. However, the closer we got to Anchorage, the lower the ceiling became. The lower ceiling had forced us to descend to twenty-five hundred feet by the time we approached Merrill Field Airport, our destination for landing. As we were on our final approach to the general-aviation runway, we noticed that Merrill had three distinctively different landing options, all parallel to one another.

Although we were heading to the general-aviation runway, to our immediate right was a very long strip of water designed to accept float planes. And to the right of the float plane runway was a large landing strip for commercial airliners. We learned later that in the winter, the float plane runway also accommodates airplanes equipped with skis when the water freezes and snow accumulates. We continued inbound for an uneventful landing, fueled and parked the airplane, and checked into the Mush Inn across from the airport for the night. We would get our rental car in the morning.

Our motel room was directly over a boiler room and never cooled down throughout the night. In the morning we decided to change hotels and checked into the Merrill Field Motel essentially next door before breakfast. Right after breakfast we called a cab, took our things to the new motel, and continued on to the airport. Our plan for that day was to fly down the Kenai Peninsula to sightsee glaciers from the air and return to Anchorage for the night.

When we departed Merrill Field Airport, the ceiling was relatively low – on the order of four thousand feet – and was broken to overcast. By now, however, we were becoming more accustomed to flying at lower altitudes. We flew along the western coastline until we were in the southern region of the Kenai Peninsula, and then we turned east to the Harding Icefield, which encompasses over three hundred square miles and spawns upward of forty glaciers. As we approached the ice field from the west, the clouds to the east of it were dissipating, allowing the diffuse light to render the ice in an incredible greenish-blue glow. We made several passes by the glacial terminus and got some fabulous photos.

Before we departed Anchorage that morning, we had decided that after our in-flight explorations we would land at the small town of Seldovia to have lunch and to walk around a bit. There was no special reason for that selection other than that it was near the southern tip of the peninsula, and it looked interesting. However, as was our practice throughout this Alaskan trip, we would typically first fly over an unfamiliar airport prior to attempting to land. We would do this to assess the runway conditions not only for landing there but also for takeoff. And that was especially relevant for the twenty-one-hundred-foot runway at Seldovia. On our first pass over the runway, we noticed that it was gravel. And because of the recent bout of wet weather experienced in that region, it looked a bit like loose gravel. When we had taken off from Merrill that morning, we seemed to have required more runway than expected, and that runway was asphalt. I keyed the mike for the radio set to our common frequency with Gordon and suggested that Seldovia's twenty-one-hundred-foot gravel runway may be a bit too marginal for our airplanes. Gordon agreed and proposed that, instead, we continue on to Homer, which is located across the Kachemak Bay from Seldovia.

We completed our overflight of Seldovia and turned back north to line up for Homer. Landing at Homer on its sixty-seven-hundred-foot asphalt runway was a much better choice. As we were flying over Kachemak Bay approaching Homer from the north, we noticed that farther to the south and toward the east, the ceiling had become considerably lower, developing a fairly scuddy condition of poor visibility. Furthermore, the surrounding mountains were all obscured. We would have to pay attention to this weather condition to see how it would develop, lest it affect our return trip to Anchorage.

We touched down at Homer, where I executed probably my best landing of the entire trip. We got a taxi that dropped us off at the town center, and we had lunch at a local coffee shop.

Afterward we walked around exploring the town and visited a small museum before returning to the airport.

Penny flew us back to Merrill in Anchorage while I daydreamed and observed the fantastic passing scenery. I was staring out the side window, mesmerized by the rugged terrain with its display of countless marshy ponds and serpentine streams, interrupted occasionally by inlet waterways penetrating from the bay. Once we had landed and parked our plane, we picked up our rental car and checked into our motel. We then splurged for dinner at one of the better restaurants. We had a great day!

After breakfast the next day, we all decided that it would be fun and interesting to further explore the Kanai Peninsula by driving over to Seward on the peninsula's eastern coast. The weather was not favorable for flying anyway, as the system we had noted in Homer the day before was arriving in Anchorage. We left Anchorage and drove along the northern coast of the Turnagain Arm of the Cook Inlet for a stop at Portage to look at the Portage Glacier. The weather made a turn for the worse, becoming rainy with generally lower, overcast skies the farther up the inlet we went. By the time we arrived at the Portage Glacier, we were greeted by a damp cold that was worsened by wind and rain. We drove over to the pier on Portage Lake where a ferry was shuttling passengers back and forth to the base of the glacier. Because of the adverse weather, we opted not to take the ferry and drove back to the visitor center.

When we parked the car and were getting our coats out of the trunk, the car keys inadvertently fell from Gordon's shirt pocket and into the trunk without his seeing it happen. Then we closed the trunk. Fortunately, we noticed they were missing before we locked the car, and we kept the car unlocked while we searched for them. When we couldn't immediately find the keys, we suspected that they likely were locked in the trunk. I was able to get into the back seat of the car and pull one of the vertical seat cushions off to expose access to the trunk. And there were the keys! With a bit of a struggle, I was able to reach them. All this time it was cold, windy, and rainy, and we were out in it. I'm not sure what we would have done if we had locked the car entirely. With the panic now subsiding, we then walked over to the visitor center to learn more about the glacier. While there, we were treated to several interesting exhibits, including a documentary on the history of this retreating glacier.

We left the visitor center and continued on to Seward, where we had lunch on the wharf. Seward appeared to be primarily a fishing town. The weather there was unchanged from what we had been experiencing all day – obviously an influence from Prince William Sound. After lunch, we wandered around the shopping area, bought a T-shirt, and left. It never really stopped raining until we left the inlet on the way back to Anchorage. This was actually a very long day with all the driving over relatively narrow and winding roads in generally rainy weather.

It was nearly midnight and becoming dusk by the time we arrived at our motel. It was also the night of the Perseids meteor shower, which we may have seen were it not for a sky filled with broken and variable overcast clouds. But the full moon likely would have drowned it out anyway.

We awoke the next morning to weather conditions that were more favorable to flying than we had experienced the day before. The ceiling was higher, and it was not raining. After we had finished breakfast, we checked out of the motel, took our stuff over to the planes, and repacked. From there, we stopped by the flight service station to see what the weather was like at Manley Hot Springs and Bettles. Our destination for the day was Manley Hot Springs, which is located approximately one hundred miles directly north of Denali National Park. The flight conditions were generally VFR – by Alaskan standards. We then drove downtown to buy a few souvenirs and return the rental car, and the receptionist took us back to the airport.

We took off from Merrill Field for Manley Hot Springs on one of the special Merrill departures that took us on a route through the city of Anchorage unlike anything we had ever experienced in the lower forty-eight. We left the airport with instructions to climb to an altitude not to exceed six hundred feet until we were across the bay north of the city. We leveled off at five hundred feet to be on the safe side. The purpose for this pattern, we suspected, was to avoid traffic interference with the nearby Anchorage International Airport. But flying over city streets and looking up at the taller buildings is something we simply don't do in the lower forty-eight! After we crossed the bay, we got on approach control for traffic advisories until reaching the first VOR navigational aid, where we were cut loose. We then climbed to twenty-five hundred feet, which we maintained as our en route altitude. We were initially exposed to scattered clouds that became overcast around Denali with bottoms around four thousand feet. And again, it was a little windy through Windy Pass!

I was in the left seat for this flight, and partway along our route we had a most interesting experience. We were still south of Denali and Windy Pass when we saw what looked like an airplane headlight coming directly toward us. Both of us spotted it. While we were discussing which direction would be best for us to turn in order to take evasive action, the wings of the on-coming "airplane" suddenly flapped. What we were looking at was the head of a bald eagle! Later on during the trip we mentioned this incident to one of the local bush pilots. He told us that this was a fairly common experience but for us to be careful if it happened again. Eagles are predators, and they don't readily back away from what they recognize as other birds. A bird strike with an eagle is always a threat.

We continued on to the airport at Manley Hot Springs, which was a twenty-eight-hundred-foot dirt runway along the Tanana River and located about five hundred feet directly in front of the Manley Roadhouse where we would be staying. The roadhouse was a stately old building built in 1906 with multiple guest rooms, a restaurant, and a bar. The town name of Hot Springs was derived from a local geothermal area that provided thermal heating to many of the buildings in the area, including the Manley Roadhouse.

As we approached the runway at the Manley Airport, the clouds became scattered to broken with bases not much higher than pattern altitude. Gordon had just made a pass over the field to inspect the runway by the time we arrived behind him. The wind sock was drooped, so we both opted for Runway 2, which allowed us to approach from the river and land toward the roadhouse. Gordon landed while we were on the downwind leg. We were on a right downwind instead of the conventional left downwind because of a fairly high hill on the left. When we turned to the base leg, however, we were blown through our proper alignment for final with what felt like a tailwind. As a result, we approached too fast and were not descending properly, so we did a go-around. The next time around, we extended our downwind leg and lined up better. The firm runway ensured a smooth landing. We parked and headed to the office to check in at the roadhouse.

On our way to the office we all noticed the outdoor "facility" positioned adjacent the area where we parked our airplanes. It was a classic outhouse with the half-moon cut in the partially open door. The toilet seat was fashioned from a two-inch-thick section of Styrofoam. All four of us laughed at this sight, as it conjured up the famous metaphor for extreme cold – a steel toilet seat in the Klondike. We figured Manley was close enough to the Klondike to count.

Ours was a quaint room with single beds and a bathroom down the hall. The leg of one of the beds was set upon a book to even the bed against a warp on the floor. In fact, the overall environment of the roadhouse was reminiscent of another century. After we all settled in to our rooms, we met back in the lounge where the lady who had checked us in gave us a bit of history of the inn and of this area. A few years earlier, the winter temperature one month had dropped to nearly −80°F for almost six weeks. Weather conditions like that, although rare, are potentially life-threatening. Most houses lost their water supply due to freezing, and residents whose houses were heated by oil found that the oil was so cold it wouldn't flow. During this period of extreme cold, Alaska was also experiencing extremely high barometric pressures, exceeding 36 inHg. The FAA was forced to initiate a special waiver regarding how flights would be handled for conditions where barometric pressures exceeded that which could be set on altimeters. Adding to this misery was the ice fog. The ice fog that formed during this cold period was extremely dense, and the combination of the high atmospheric pressure and low temperature was such that chimneys wouldn't draw. When coupled with the long periods of darkness that occur during the winter months, the environment was extremely oppressive. People living in the surrounding environs came to the inn as a place to survive the emergency. The roadhouse, with its geothermal heating, provided both shelter and comfort for everyone during these extreme conditions.

We learned that Fairbanks was 170 miles from there, and at least at the time of our visit, all but about 25 of these miles were dirt roads. Because of this nearly extreme isolation, most of the residents have emergency first aid training. Any instance of life- or limb-threatening injuries would qualify for – and rely upon – army medivac helicopter support.

We had dinner at the inn, after which Gordon and I went for a walk to look for the enclosure where the hot springs broke through the surface. We had been informed earlier that it was closed, but we were curious about the general layout. Because it had rained the previous day and had sprinkled a little after we arrived, the air was cool and damp and the roads had a thin top layer of mud. We walked around and took a few photos of the area.

We were farther north now, and at eleven thirty it was still twilight. Our goal for the following day was to fly to Bettles, located above the Arctic Circle. If all were to go well, I wanted to see if we could get as far north as Deadhorse so that we could say we flew over the coastline of the Arctic Ocean. But the weather patterns would dictate whether or not we could make this attempt.

The weather gods were frowning on us as we awoke the following morning. It was raining with a low overcast. Since we weren't going anywhere in that kind of weather, we took our time getting up and having breakfast. The roadhouse dining room setup was somewhat of a family style, which allowed for a leisurely pace without inconveniencing the waitstaff. We dallied most of the morning, taking our time while waiting for the rain to stop. And by mid to late morning, it did and the clouds began to dissipate. We called flight service for a weather outlook for Bettles and learned that conditions likely would be improving over the next couple of hours. We then went for a walk along one of the dirt roads for about an hour. Once back from our walk we filed our flight plan as a flight of two, did our preflight, and departed.

Because of the recent rain and the fact that the runway was dirt, we executed a soft-field takeoff as a precaution. This went very smoothly, as there was hardly any awareness of runway surface roughness. As we climbed out, we noticed that the expanse of cloud covering was in reality much more scattered and dissipating faster than it appeared to be on the ground. So we headed north over the rolling hills. In about ten minutes we were intersecting the Yukon River, which we followed for a while to the point where the Alaska pipeline crossed it. After several photos of the pipeline-river interface, we banked the airplane to put the Bettles ADF needle to its nose. This new position turned out also to be the general direction of the pipeline and its support road, so we followed it all the way to Bettles.

Vegetation became more sparse the farther north we went, and the evidence of permafrost grew more obvious. The occasional clump of white birch trees were looking rather stunted, and we were becoming a bit caviler flying at low altitudes. The slight elevation gain south of Bettles forced us to climb all the way up to thirty-three hundred feet – high by Alaskan standards!

Bettles had a nice, well-compacted gravel runway. On our approach to land, however, a helicopter raced us in for landing. We later talked with the pilot who told us he had always wanted to beat a Mooney. We retorted that it wasn't a fair race, as we were slowing down to land. We fueled up, parked our planes, and got the very last of the available rooms in the six-room Bettles Lodge.

Since we arrived around noon, we had a quick lunch, after which we walked over to the flight service building on the field to get a weather outlook for points along the North Slope. On our way over, we passed by our parked airplanes, where we stopped and looked over the airfield. While we were standing there, another pilot walked by. He commented that he had never seen two airplanes with retractable landing gear up here above the Arctic Circle. We laughed at that and told him that those planes were ours.

When we received our weather outlook for the North Slope, we learned that the forecast predicting VFR with a forty-five-hundred foot ceiling was somewhat favorable for Deadhorse, but Barrow was calling for a fifteen-hundred-foot overcast with occasional breaks in it. Neither of these conditions sounded overly favorable to us, so we decided to check again in the morning to see if it would be possible by then for us to make it farther north.

The primary reason these weather conditions seemed marginal for us was the following. To get to either Deadhorse or Barrow, we would have to fly across the Brooks Range, a seven-hundred-mile east-west range with peak elevations approaching nine thousand feet. A forty-five-thousand-foot ceiling would mean we would need to fly IFR. But the reported freezing level was around five thousand feet, and neither of our planes were equipped for deicing. If we were to make this flight, we would have to be VFR and fly under the clouds. While discussing these options, we reminded ourselves of the ill-fated flight of Wiley Post and Will Rogers on August 15, 1935, when their airplane crashed on takeoff from a lagoon near Point Barrow. Bad weather had caused them to be unsure of their position, and they had landed on the lagoon to ask directions. Unfortunately, the engine failed on takeoff, and the nose-heavy airplane flipped over and landed inverted, killing both occupants.

The adjacent building associated with the lodge also served as a restaurant, and as one might expect, it was fairly small, with only a few tables. The menu, however, was pretty much limited to what the chef was fixing that day, and that evening it was hamburgers. But to us that really didn't matter, as we were hungry.

While we were having dinner, we again met up with the helicopter pilot. We told him of our thoughts of possibly flying up to the North Slope and asked whether he had ever done that. He said he had and then went on to describe the safest way for us to do it. As we had already assumed, he suggested that we best stay VFR for this flight. But there was a pass due north of where we were that people flying out of Bettles typically take. Unfortunately, the pass is somewhat Z shaped, and one can't see the cloud conditions on the far side of the mountain until well after entering the pass. And the pass is fairly narrow. He suggested that when we enter the pass, we fly fairly close to one side of it. That would give us sufficient room to quickly turn around if we found that the far side was obscured by clouds or fog after rounding the bend. That did not sound at all encouraging.

The one remaining room at the Bettles Lodge had beds for only three people, but this was not a problem as we had planned for such an eventuality. I volunteered to sleep on the floor in one of the sleeping bags we had brought. Even with all four of us somewhat sandwiched into the room, we generally slept well. The weather outside when we woke up was low overcast with fog obscuring the mountains. It had rained during the night.

Since our room also had a kitchenette, we made breakfast with the camping supplies we had aboard our planes. Immediately after breakfast, we repacked the planes and went over to the flight service station. Aircraft were flying into and leaving Bettles already. We once again checked the weather conditions for the North Slope at both Deadhorse and Barrow. It had been foggy there for the last several weeks, which is normal, but Deadhorse was actually reporting clear conditions, while Barrow still had a fifteen-hundred-foot ceiling. However, the Brooks Range that we had to cross was completely obscured, and the weather would be deteriorating at Bettles later in the day.

After discussing our options, we concluded that it would not be wise to even attempt a flight to the North Slope. If it were necessary to file IFR just to get there, that would defeat the whole purpose of going. We would miss all the surrounding scenery. Being able to fly VFR was the primary motivation to go in the first place. And if we did make the flight, we would have to return to Bettles to refuel before continuing east. But with the weather closing in at Bettles, even if we made it through the pass in the Brooks Range, there was a real possibility that we could be trapped on the other side and forced into an IFR flight back to Bettles. Nobody liked that idea with the present reported freezing level of thirty-five hundred to five thousand feet and the clouds full of moisture. So we decided instead to continue on to Circle Hot Springs but swing northeast over the foothills of the Brooks Range to the Chandalar River and follow it to Fort Yukon. From there we would continue on to Circle Hot Springs, which was southeast of Fort Yukon by sixty some-odd miles.

Everything went smoothly as we left Bettles, and it was Penny's turn in the left seat. As we departed the airport and turned to a left downwind, we had a bald eagle join us off our right wing. From the right seat I could easily make out his curved yellow beak and dark eyes. We flew in formation with the eagle for a short time until our speed increased sufficiently that the eagle couldn't keep up. But for a moment, we and the eagle were flying together as one.

The ceiling was relatively low, around four thousand feet, so we leveled off at twenty-five hundred feet. We joked to each other over the radio that it was almost oxygen-requirement altitude by Alaskan standards! The clouds were definitely settled heavily over the mountains, and we got a few photos of this. After about ten minutes or so we intersected the Alaskan pipeline where it comes through the Brooks Range. And this is where we had decided earlier to look for the canyon that would lead us to the Chandalar River. It's not unusual in the world of aviation to find that what one sees looking out the window differs from what one sees on a chart. Visibility wasn't necessarily marginal, but it was a little scuddy along the mountain ridges. We had to decide which canyon to enter and which stream to follow through which narrow pass with the descending ceiling and intermittent rain that would lead to the Chandalar River. Through this momentary confusion, we entered one pass that Gordon, who was in front of us, didn't feel good about, so we all decided we should turn around and start over. We positioned ourselves on the right-hand side of the pass at different altitudes so we wouldn't accidently run into each other when turning around in the rain. In the course of the confusion, we ended up as the front airplane and flew back to the pipeline to use as a point of reference to start over again. As it turned out, we were only about five minutes from it. This time we followed the charts more closely, picked our way through a different canyon, found the Chandalar River, and followed it to the Yukon River and Fort Yukon.

As we approached Fort Yukon, the clouds had begun to dissipate, and visibility became virtually unlimited. The vastness of the Yukon River flood plain with its wide wandering rivulets running parallel to the main river portrayed a breathtaking sight. There were thousands of ponds and smaller bodies of water sitting atop the permafrost as far as the eye could see. The nearly flat terrain was virtually devoid of trees, with the only vegetation being strains of lichens tolerant of a marshy environment that would be frozen over for most of the year. Everywhere we looked as we passed over this stunningly incredible scene, we witnessed an unchanged natural wonder for hundreds of square miles. We commented at the time that it was extremely unlikely that any human had ever walked across this surface.

With the improved visibility and fairly flat terrain, we spotted Circle Hot Springs from several miles away. Its name is derived from the fact that it is located virtually on the Arctic Circle. The approach into the airport tended to favor Runway 26. Since the

Mooney that Gordon and Shirley were in was a little faster than ours, they had passed us, so Gordon approached first. He wasn't set up right, so he did a go-around and ended up behind us. Penny lined up well and did a very nice landing. Gordon followed us in.

By the time we were parking, a van from the hotel had already arrived. We loaded everything we needed for the night into the van and were taken to the hotel. The rooms were quite reasonably priced, but the hotel required cash. Unfortunately, our cash was getting low, as we tend not to carry much. But we had enough on us to cover the night, so we checked in, after which we wandered about the area.

We had dinner in a local saloon with walls covered with autographed dollar bills, a tradition started by an old miner back in the 1930s who would tack a dollar on the wall when he left to go prospecting. When he returned, if he had been lucky, he would buy drinks with his gold. If not, he would buy them with the dollar he had tacked on the wall. Saloon patrons now joined the tradition and left their own autographed dollar bills.

When we awoke the following morning, we commented on the glow we had seen in the north at midnight the night before from the sun's being barely below the horizon. We then had breakfast at the hotel, called flight service, and checked out. Because of our location so far out in the bush, we opened our flight plan over the phone with instructions to update our position over Eagle, our last reporting point in Alaska before crossing into Canada. We checked out and got a ride to the airport. While at Circle Hot Springs, we learned that this was the very first airport in Alaska to become operational.

After preflight, we taxied to the departure end of the runway for a smooth soft-field takeoff. We again climbed to twenty-five hundred feet and headed due east to intersect the Yukon River and fly on to Dawson, our destination. We turned upstream, which was south, and followed it. The sky became more overcast the farther south we went, and lenticular clouds were forming. Lenticular clouds, with their very characteristic lens shape, are of special concern to general-aviation pilots as they are typically indicators of significant turbulence. The weather briefing we had received prior to our departure that morning had reported local severe turbulence south of Dawson, with Dawson being overcast with light rain. Meanwhile, at our location, the ceilings were still greater than four thousand feet. We continued along the Yukon maintaining twenty-five hundred feet, following the bends in the river through the canyons.

We reported in to Northway Radio as we approached Eagle and got updated instructions for our arrival at the Dawson airport, one of which was to call in when we were fifteen miles out. We arrived in Dawson City, Yukon, at midafternoon after the fairly long flight from Circle Hot Springs. I was in the left seat for this flight, and the flight conditions were fairly good. Although there was a solid overcast ceiling, it was still greater than four thousand feet and visibility was at least five miles.

Dawson City is located on the Yukon River at the base of the mountains on both of its sides. Dawson was a small village of barely five hundred people at the start of the 1896 gold rush. By the summer of 1898, however, the population had swollen to over forty thousand. But the gold rush didn't last all that long, and by 1912 the town numbers had diminished to barely two thousand. Its population today is not quite fourteen hundred. Nonetheless, an estimated million and a quarter pounds of gold have been taken out of the Klondike area.

The Dawson airport was six miles out of town up a canyon following the Klondike River, which itself empties into the Yukon. We flew up the canyon about five hundred feet above pattern altitude right behind Gordon and Shirley. To our amazement, we noticed that several gold-mining operations with modern dredging equipment were still ongoing in the Klondike. From the air it appeared that every pebble and every grain of sand throughout the total river had at one time been churned over. The entire river has been dredged, from where it empties into the Yukon to upstream well past the airport. Yet gold is still being found.

Shirley was in the left seat of their Mooney and put her landing gear down before I did, so while I was looking out the window at the extensive hydraulic mining of the river, I was gaining a bit. When I realized that, I promptly put our gear down and backed off. When we spotted the airport, we were already set up for the base leg for Runway 02. I did a 360-degree turn while Shirley landed, and then we landed right afterward. Since we had entered Canada from Alaska and this was our first stop, we taxied over to customs. Once again we had an easy time being processed.

Because of our fairly long flight, we needed fuel and taxied to the fuel pump. But there we were presented with a temporary problem. We learned, fortunately from a pilot who had already arrived at the fuel pump prior to us, that because it was a Sunday, the fuel station was unattended. And in order to get fuel, there was a call-out fee of thirty dollars that had to be paid. Luckily, when he called, he was able to find an available person who was checked out with the fuel system and had a key. We agreed to split the call-out cost with him. However, when the fuel attendant arrived, he indicated that he had to be paid in cash only. Because we had to pay cash at the Circle Hot Springs hotel, I didn't have quite enough cash remaining to completely fill our plane. But fortunately we were able to get enough fuel to make it to our next destination. Our plan for the next day was to continue on to Whitehorse. After gassing up, we parked and walked over to the airport lobby.

While Penny was on the phone getting us a hotel, the rest of us were talking with a local miner who was in the airport lobby waiting for his flight. He told us that there was still a lot of gold being taken out of the Klondike area. He said that he had arrived there with a crew that past spring to dig some old claims, but their intent was to dig through and below the permafrost that earlier miners were never able to get to. He mentioned that they didn't strike anything until June. But when they did, they found enough gold to pay back all of their investment. Their method was to dredge through the permafrost with heavy construction equipment and placer mine the result.

We were greeted by a dull gray sky with low-hanging scuddy clouds as we awoke the next morning. The feeling of dampness that permeated the room was intensified by a drizzling rain that fell on the unpaved street below our hotel window. A lone pedestrian with his jacket pulled above his head to shield himself from the mist hurried along the board sidewalk. The morning, at least, was not showing great promise of its being an ideal day to continue the next leg of our flight to begin our return home from our flying adventures through Alaska.

The scuddy morning definitely didn't look very encouraging. But the previous night before going to bed, we had decided to meet at eight for breakfast and afterward explore some of the highlights of this historic gold-mining town. There was a recitation to be given on Robert Service later that morning, and we were all interested in sitting in on that. Robert Service was the undisputed Bard of the Yukon. The classics "The Cremation of Sam McGee" and "The Shooting of Dan McGrew" are among his best known poems.

The recitation was to be held in the cabin that Robert Service once occupied, so after breakfast we ventured out into the misty rain over the muddy streets of Dawson and up the wood boardwalk to its location. We arrived in ample time to claim good seats. The recitation was given by Thomas Byrne, a Scotsman, and it was an excellent presentation. He told the story of Robert Service's life and recited "Dan McGrew," "Sam McGee," and various other selected verses. It lasted about an hour and a half.

When we left the presentation, we found a telephone and Gordon called Transport Canada for a weather outlook for our planned flight to Whitehorse. At the time of the call, the ceiling was low and nebulous, and visibility was marginal. Although it was only mid-August, the freezing level onset again began at a fairly low altitude, and we all agreed that it would be unwise to fly to Whitehorse under IFR. Our required altitude would be fairly high, and with the considerable moisture contained within the clouds, the probability of our experiencing icing conditions would be a near certainty. As I mentioned earlier, neither of our airplanes was equipped for deicing. But Gordon was told that a clearing trend was expected for around midafternoon, so we decided to check out of our rooms with hopes that the local ceiling would rise sufficiently by then for us to take off. Whitehorse was already reporting a four-thousand-foot ceiling and was expecting conditions to improve later to scattered clouds and a forty-mile visibility.

So we explored Dawson and all of its gold-rush era highlights. We looked in on Diamond Tooth Gerties Gambling Hall to see what that entailed. Although the building had been erected relatively recently, having opened in 1971, it was built in the style of the era of the Klondike gold rush. Vaudeville shows are held daily during tourist season. We then meandered over to the cabin where Jack London spent one winter at the height of the gold rush and investigated that. As we wandered through town, we found the old-fashioned board sidewalks to be quite unusual. But they were sufficient to keep us off the muddy streets, and we were grateful for that. We later learned in our explorations that one of America's greatest theater tycoons, Alexander Pantages, got his start in Dawson in a small theater he opened there. His name is likely better associated with the famous Pantages Theater located on Hollywood Boulevard in Hollywood.

We continued walking around Dawson until about midafternoon, when the ceiling did indeed rise. The earlier scuddiness was dissipating nicely, and we had clear visibility for several miles. So we returned to the hotel, collected our luggage, and got a ride to the airport. After a very thorough weather briefing from the Dawson flight service, which included several pilot reports, we decided that for the majority of the flight we would stay low and fly directly over the river. That scheme would guarantee to keep us away from high terrain, even with a fairly low ceiling. We were finally in the air a little after four o'clock. By then the ceiling had risen to around four thousand feet and the sun was breaking through. It was Penny's turn to take the left seat and fly.

We climbed out and flew fairly low following the Klondike River, and we turned left over Dawson and out onto the Yukon. The south bank of the Yukon offered a spectacular view of the steep hillsides lining the river. The reflections of the streamers of sunbeams breaking through the clouds at the convolution of the Klondike and Yukon Rivers presented us with a dramatic sight and a promise of clearing conditions ahead. The ultrafine silt, or glacial flour, of the Klondike does not immediately mix with the relatively clear waters of the Yukon, and what appears from the air is the illusion of two separate rivers flowing side by side. We had witnessed this phenomenon numerous times throughout our Arctic adventure, and this condition continues for miles downstream of the merging rivers.

We turned left and followed the Yukon upstream while climbing to about twenty-five hundred feet. We had a distance of nearly three hundred nautical miles to cover, which we estimated would take us nearly two and a half hours. Gordon and Shirley's airplane was a bit faster than ours, so they were in front. Because our ceiling was well below mountain peaks that jutted abruptly above us, often with fairly steep banks, we tended to navigate primarily toward the center of the river. Even though the Yukon is a fairly wide river, the canyon walls on both sides and the overcast ceiling above us gave us the sensation that we were flying through a tunnel. It was a bit eerie at first, especially as we passed through occasional periods of rain showers, but we got used to it.

The Yukon is the third longest river in North America, and with its origins in British Columbia it's the longest river in Yukon and Alaska. Its source is generally accepted to be the Llewellyn Glacier at Atlin Lake, although there are several other contributors. The section of the river over which we were flying was sufficiently wide that, were we to meet an oncoming airplane, we would have ample clearance to avoid any danger. Near the town of Whitehorse is a cascade of rapids on the Yukon River resembling the flowing manes of galloping horses, and it's from this display that the town derives its name.

Before we took off from Dawson, the four of us had once more agreed upon an unassigned radio communication frequency that both planes could use for us to stay in contact, and we chatted with each other all along the way. Our plan was to leave the Yukon River at the town of Carmacks and follow the road to Whitehorse. The river continues to meander from that direction anyway, where it forms Lake Laberge and joins the road just north of Whitehorse. This is the very same Lake Laberge whose banks upon Robert Service had reported that Sam McGee was cremated, although he misspelled it in his poem. The correct spelling is *Laberge*, with an *e*. But that doesn't rhyme well with *marge*, as in "that night on the marge of Lake Labarge …" where he spelled it with an *a*.

The weather had cleared considerably more, and slight turbulence was picking up the closer we got to Whitehorse. As we approached the lake, we took a few photographs and I recited the first stanza of Robert Service's famous poem over the radio to our flight partners. It seemed only appropriate.

The changing weather at Whitehorse had brought with it some fairly strong winds with gusts to twenty-five knots, and the winds were spilling down the mountains located immediately west of the airport. As a result, the airport traffic advisory was recommending that we land on the shorter runway that runs nearly perpendicular to the primary north-south runways and crosses both, as that would give us our desired headwind for landing. But the Whitehorse airport is located atop a fairly steep cliff, over two hundred feet above the town and Yukon River below, and the threshold of the runway we were to land on is very close to the edge of that cliff. When the winds are as strong from the west as they were when we arrived, and with the air rolling down the adjoining mountains and over the edge of a cliff as we expected they were, the atmosphere acts like an invisible waterfall. This condition presents an inherent danger to landing aviators, as severe downdrafts are possible. An airplane is quite vulnerable to being affected by this when power is being reduced and it's descending. Unless one plans for such an occurrence, one could be looking up at the edge of the cliff at the last moment! That is not an ideal position for an airplane. So when we approached for the landing, Penny kept the airplane relatively high in anticipation of this event. And sure enough, the downdraft put us right at the altitude we needed to be, and she made a perfect landing.

We taxied for fuel behind our friends' Mooney, and then we each parked the airplanes. Our parking area was across from a lone Bonanza that had arrived shortly before we had. Something seemed amiss with that plane, so the four of us walked over to it. As we got closer, we noticed that it was almost entirely covered with clear ice, some of which was as much as a quarter-inch thick. The same FBO facility where we bought gas also rented rooms, so when we checked in, we asked about the Bonanza. The clerk told us that it too had started out from Dawson as a flight of two, but the pilots had decided to go IFR. Because of the necessity to be at a much higher altitude, both Bonanzas got into severe icing conditions. One airplane went down and was lost, and it had not yet been found at the time of our inquiry. The other had arrived an hour or so before we did, completely iced over. The four of us looked at one another and nodded that we had made a wise choice for deciding to wait until the ceiling lifted.

As we discussed earlier, all icing conditions are hazardous to aircraft, but some are much more serious than others. There are two primary varieties of icing: rime ice and clear ice. And clear ice is the worse. Rime ice tends to be crystalline and sloughs off fairly easily. If the two Bonanzas had encountered only rime ice, possibly both planes could have made it. But clear ice bonds to surfaces and doesn't readily break up. While rime ice may slough off, there is virtually no recovery from clear ice without deicing equipment. Throughout the remainder of our trip home we continued to inquire if there had been any news of the missing Bonanza. We heard nothing.

We checked into our room and dropped off our luggage. Then all of us met to decide where we would go for dinner. As we left the FBO on our way to the restaurant, we stopped to admire what we all mutually agreed was the world's most unique wind sock – a now-decommissioned but once-operational DC-3 that was carefully suspended off the ground, balanced on a spindle. It sat above its balance point with its landing gear fully extended as if approaching to land. It was so delicately perched upon its pivot that it responded to a mere five-knot wind. As it boasted to be, it was indeed the world's largest weather vane!

We took several photos of this marvel and then headed off to the restaurant. At dinner we learned that Mount Spurr, a volcano located about eighty miles west of Anchorage, had erupted, plunging the city into premature darkness. The ash coated the streets with a quarter inch of dust and forced the closure of all the city's airports. We were fortunate that our plans called for us to leave Anchorage when we did.

There's good news and bad news about overnight stays at an airport FBO. The good news is that it's extremely convenient, as it's walking distance from where the plane is parked. It's relatively inexpensive when compared with motel rates, and a courtesy car is typically offered to guests to drive into town for dinner. The bad news, however, is that these accommodations are places of business and can be very noisy, especially if the building is constructed primarily of sheet metal. That was our experience in Whitehorse.

We were awakened that morning around four thirty to a cacophony of commotion. It sounded like someone had dropped an anvil overhead and then kept tripping over it. After much tossing and turning for the next two or three hours, we finally got up and had breakfast in the pilot's lounge.

After breakfast, we checked out and got our flight weather briefing. Our destination was Fort St. John, British Columbia, and the weather projections looked good but with anticipated light to moderate turbulence. We took off from Whitehorse and headed southeast over the Alaska Highway, anticipating about a four-plus-hour flight. However, by the time we got to Watson Lake, which was about an hour and a half out, the coffee hit bottom, and all four of us decided we couldn't make the entire trip without a bathroom break – so we landed and went. With a great feeling of relief, we were off again and headed for Fort St. John, this time continuing all the way.

A few clouds began to gather as we got underway, but they generally remained only scattered and mostly below us. However, one cloud segment of about a half mile in width was solid beneath us. Although we could see the ground ahead of us, we were for a few minutes technically flying what is called VFR on top. That means that the visibility around the aircraft is virtually unlimited, but the pilot can't see the ground directly below because of the cloud cover. By US aviation rules, this flight condition is very common and is done all the time. By Canadian aviation rules, however, it is illegal. Canada does not allow flights that are VFR on top. If one is above the clouds, regardless of visibility, one must file IFR and be on an instrument flight plan. This rule is for the pilot's own safety. When one considers the vastness of the Canadian wilderness, one can easily understand how a pilot with rusty navigation skills could easily get off course and become lost. So for a few minutes, we were flying illegally.

We picked up a very good tailwind en route and also found the turbulence the weather briefer told us to expect. And it was indeed moderate at times. We were not disappointed! After enjoying the scenery along the way, thanks to the great visibility, we spotted the Fort St. John airport. We called for our landing instructions and landed.

We refueled, checked in, and arranged for itinerant parking for the night. That was the first time we had heard the term *itinerant* used in place of *transient*, but it means the same. The FBO manager recommended the Cedar Lodge Motor Inn, a local motel that would pick us up from the airport. We called them and then went to the pilot's lounge to wait for our ride. While there, we struck up a conversation with another pilot who was also waiting for a ride. He had stayed at the same FBO in Whitehorse as we had but a couple of days earlier. He had even helped the owner install a washer and dryer. We told him of our moderate disappointment at not being able to get to Barrow or Deadhorse on the North Slope, and he replied that he had just returned from there. He said that the entire area was overcast, and it typically stays overcast for months at a time. All the time he was there, the ceiling was only five hundred feet. He had flown an Apache twin all over the North Slope at an altitude of three hundred feet. That would be a bit low for us, even by Alaskan VFR standards.

The next morning we met fairly early for breakfast, as we wanted to get an early start. Our ultimate goal for the day was to see how far south we could get, ideally all the way to Klamath Falls, Oregon, to stop for the night; so the day would involve a lot of flying. We must have done something right, as the weather gods were good to us again. The skies would be clear for the entire route, and we would be getting a slight tailwind – weather conditions that were just the opposite of what we had experienced on our way north. We filed our flight plan to Bellingham, Washington, where we would have to land to clear US customs.

We left Fort St. John heading for Mackenzie at the end of Williston Lake on our way to Prince George, following the remainder of the Alaska Highway. South of Prince George we picked up the Fraser River to follow it through the various canyons it cut on its way south. We had originally planned to do something similar on the way north, but because of the hard overcast at the time, we were forced to fly IFR and stay on the airway. The canyons cut by the Fraser River were narrow, steep, and spectacular, and the river itself churned through numerous rapids. We flew as low as we dared so we could still have room to maneuver if need be as we came around bends. There were times when we were not very far from the tops of the ridges.

The river wended its way to the town of Hope and then turned west into a wide, steep valley. Because of the presence of the mountains west of the Fraser River along much of its route, the terrain itself seemed quite arid in parts. The mountains encompassing Hope and the streams and other rivers flowing by it gave the town a very alpine look, much like a Swiss setting. Flying west from there put us suddenly into civilization, with the abrupt appearance of all the farms and small towns. We tuned in the Bellingham, Washington, NDB and headed toward it. We landed there and taxied to the customs site to clear US customs and change pilots.

Going through customs at Bellingham was probably one of the easiest US customs experiences we have ever had, except for my having to redo my form because I had put down Bellingham as our last US town. It turns out that Circle City, Alaska, the location of Circle Hot Springs, was our last town in the United States! The customs agent laughed at this, as he said that mine was a common error made by people returning from Alaska. We tend to forget that Alaska is part of the United States. We left our planes parked at the customs site, got them refueled, and had lunch at the Bellingham terminal. During lunch, we finalized our decision to continue on to Klamath Falls as our stop for the night.

We took off from Bellingham straight out and climbing with the objective of getting over the 10,000-foot Seattle Terminal Control Area, or TCA. A TCA is a positive control airspace that surrounds all airports with heavy commercial airliner traffic, and general-aviation flights must stay out unless explicitly cleared to enter. Although we were climbing to 11,500 feet, we called for TCA clearance in the event we were not quite high enough when we reached the TCA boundary. But we made it. We also received a TCA clearance.

The visibility was incredible for the Pacific Northwest. We had never seen Seattle so clearly. We could distinguish every feature of Mount Rainier as it passed by our left wingtip. And Mount St. Helens was now looming up in front of us. Once we were well outside of the Seattle TCA, we canceled flight following with the air traffic control and flew over to Mount St. Helens. Our plan was to fly directly across the center of the crater itself, which we did. We had the most eerie feeling as we looked down at the lifeless, ashy lava plug at the crater center and watched the steamy plumes emanate from its different parts. There was definite geologic activity not all that far below us. Flying to the opposite rim seemed to take an eternity. Gordon and Shirley had flown over the crater a couple of years earlier, and they commented that the center dome was now a lot larger than it had been the last time they flew over it.

We continued on south to Eugene and then turned left to Klamath, passing over Crater Lake along the way. As we arrived into Klamath, the sun was beginning to set, the earliest sunset we had seen in a long time. We found a hotel and settled in for the night. The next day we would head south and home.

We met for breakfast at nine the next morning. Afterward, we checked out of our hotel, got a ride to the airport, did our airplane preflights, filed our flight plans, and said our goodbyes. That day, our destinations would be different.

Penny and I took off straight south with a planned stop in Modesto for fuel and to change pilots. We arrived home at six thirty that evening, tired but content after logging fifty-two hours of total flying time during a most incredible journey.

Without a doubt, our flight to Alaska was by far the greatest adventure we ever experienced over our three decades of flying. This journey brought together and challenged all of our flying and navigation skills. Navigational aids were scarce and pilotage was our course of action throughout most of the places we traveled. We followed rivers, valleys, and coastlines and flew from landmark to landmark. We encountered virtually every conceivable weather environment, save for blinding snowstorms, and had to deal with each. We faced persistent low ceilings for the majority of the trip. We flew in and out of rain squalls and low-hanging mist. And we stayed on the ground during periods when the weather was truly threatening. Once we became comfortable with "Alaskan VFR," we flew at altitudes much lower than we would ever consider in the lower forty-eight. We flew over countless pristine landscapes, terrains of intense beauty, heaths and marshes upon which we are certain no human has ever walked. We followed numerous rivers where the glacial flour from adjoining streams never mixed with the waters of the main river. Alaska is truly the final frontier, and our experience was one that very few pilots have ever undertaken. We, for a short while, were explorers.

CHAPTER 10

HOME FROM THE HEAVENS

It finally happened. In September 2017, Penny and I hung up our wings and retired from flying. After nearly thirty-four years of immersion in the aviation environment, we were reluctant to take this step. But during the previous couple of years or so leading up to this decision, we had not been accumulating the necessary flight hours we felt we should be logging in order maintain sufficient proficiency, in our minds at least. In the realm of flight, that lapse could be disastrous – even fatal.

Anyone who is presently active in the aviation world or has ever been in that domain knows that flying is not a casual endeavor. One must be on top of one's game from the takeoff roll to the final touchdown. Any anomaly occurring between those two events can't be dealt with by pulling over onto Cloud Nine and popping the hood! Being a bit rusty in that environment can have dire consequences, and such a lapse is unacceptable.

So we hung up our wings after a long and fantastic run that began in 1985. It had truly been fun, but we had come to the end of that era. The good news in this decision, however, was that we left on our own terms, not because we were forced to. We were still current with our biannual flight reviews, our medical certifications were still valid, and we'd never had an accident or an FAA violation. It was merely time to go.

Penny decided earlier that year that she would retire from flying and opted not to redo her biannual flight review, which was due in June. Her medical was good through August. When she made her decision, I was on the fence but leaning heavily toward this same decision. In June both my medical and biannual flight reviews were due. We felt that one of us needed to remain current in the event we had to demonstrate the plane when we put it up for sale. So I renewed both.

As for the airplane itself, we reluctantly sold it. Our Mooney formally left us on Tuesday, September 5, 2017. We had first bought that airplane in July 1987, so it was like losing a member of the family.

And so ended our era in aviation. It was a great run and we enjoyed every second. Throughout these pages I have presented but a sampling of our many aviation adventures. Countless others still remain untold. But I hope these selections have been sufficient to give the reader a feel for the allure of this mystical yet fascinating environment. Flying is not something one gives up lightly. But like all things in nature, this too has now faded into memory.

For a moment we played in the heavens.
For a moment we lived in the sky.
For a moment we followed its siren,
But that moment has now passed by.

We have now come down from the heavens.
We no longer play in the sky.
Our wings lie asleep in stillness,
No longer spread ready to fly.

But our minds are yet drawn skyward.
Perhaps we'll return one day.
So let's toast to the Spirit of the Sky Walkers!
Sic transit gloria mundi.

ACKNOWLEDGMENT

Anna Kelly, a superior impressionist artist and good friend, designed and painted the cover for this book. As a noteworthy coincidence in keeping with the book's theme, her father, Colonel Hua Kao "Waco" Teng, was a decorated combat pilot in the Chinese theater of World War II. Among his many duties, he flew numerous missions attached to the 375th Squadron of the 308th Bomber Group of the 14th Air Force under the command of General Claire Chennault of the "Flying Tigers" fame.

Printed in the United States
By Bookmasters